MARY C. CROWLEY'S Decorate Your Home with Love

Pictured here is the informal dining area in my home.

MARY C. CROWLEY'S Decorate Your Home with Love

Fleming H. Revell Company
Old Tappan, New Jersey

BY Mary C. Crowley

Think Mink!
Women Who Win
You Can Too
A Pocketful of Hope

Scripture quotations are from the King James Version of the Bible.

Library of Congress Cataloging-in-Publication Data

Crowley, Mary C.
    Mary C. Crowley's Decorate your home with love.

    1. Interior decoration—Handbooks, manuals, etc.
I. Title.   II. Title: Decorate your home with love.
NK2115.C96   1986   747.213   85-14604
ISBN 0-8007-1454-7

Contents

Introduction

Come On In . . .

Happy People Live Here

Warm walls that seem to hug you. Or give you a feeling of airiness that makes you want to fly. Rugs and furniture that are comfy and inviting and somehow "go together"; or tables and chairs and accessories that glow with the richness of polished wood. Splashes of sunny color that call out, "Look at me!" in pictures and plants and pillows. Patterns that charm in curtains and tablecloths, textures that literally make you tingle. Mirrors, candles, plaques, and pretty things that reflect your personality, and the interests and activities of the people you love.

Rooms that say, "Welcome—snuggle down and stay awhile! People live here who laugh and hug and listen to each other's problems. Who care and share and have a good time." It's a feeling of harmony, caring, friendliness, fun. It's done by "decorating"—and you can do it too!

Over twenty-five years ago I started a company called *Home Interiors and Gifts* with $5,000 and a belief that God was a partner all the way and wanted me to help women establish happier, more loving homes. For years I'd had a desire to help women fix up their homes to recreate God's beauty inside the house. I'd always believed that if women cared enough to make their homes attractive, they'd also care enough to make themselves attractive and become happier people.

I firmly believe that "God never takes time to make a nobody"— we're all created in God's image, with great potential and ingenuity. And as our inner knowledge that God has His hand in every single minute of our lives grows, we can stop thinking "lack" and start thinking in terms of a glowing inner self–image. A self–image of esteem and pride that can be transferred into our homes and into the lives of those we love.

Today *Home Interiors and Gifts* is one of the largest personal-sales companies in the country, with gross sales of more than $400 million. And my pride comes from knowing that we're a business that God not only helped start, but one that He keeps His hand in every single minute. As someone once said to me, "In most companies P and L mean Profit and Loss—but at *Home Interiors* they mean People and Love." We're not interested in the cold hard facts, we're interested in the warm people bene-

fits—and in our business they've been considerable! Over the years I've traveled hundreds of thousands of miles all over the country, recruiting and training new sales people, and meeting with women in all walks of life who want to make the most of the talents—and the homes—God gave them.

It's too bad that the very word *decorating* sometimes scares people. They think they don't have the time or energy or money to "decorate" their houses or apartments or cabins at the lake. Oh, books and magazines offer to help—but they too often overwhelm you with an avalanche of sometimes-mystifying instructions and too-swank settings. Or you may fear that by "decorating" you'll lose the spontaneity and homey, lived-in feeling of your surroundings.

But decorating doesn't *have* to be complicated or expensive or hoity-toity. Oh, it can be a major overhaul if your life and your budget are up to it. But it can also be just a touch here and there—a coat of paint or a cluster of candles or an old wicker chest rescued from a garage sale and slicked up with a jolly new color. Or it can mean the addition of some striking or charming new accessories—I call them "the little gems that make a big difference" and they can make your rooms sparkle without big expense or exhausting effort. They're touches added because you *care*. And after all, "Houses are made of wood and stone—but only love can make a home."

It's a love that makes a difference to everyone, no matter how old or young, no matter what situation they may be in. I was at one of our shows where some of our items were displayed in a room setting we had assembled. A little boy, about nine or ten, came up with his mother and looked and looked at all our pretty accessories and furnishings. He just stood there for the longest time. And finally he said, "I wish we could have my Scout meetings here." He was drawn to that room and the atmosphere it conveyed—and his mother was more surprised than anyone at his reaction. "I never thought he noticed things like that," she said. But he did. Children *do*.

I once received a letter from a nurse in Maine telling me how one of our *Home Interiors* representatives (we call them Displayers) had continued to bring gifts to an elderly woman she'd met in the hospital, who had no family or visitors otherwise. The ill woman's name was Lorena, and the brass candleholder and candles brought by our Displayer did wonders to cheer her up and make her hospital room seem more of a home. Before her death Lorena announced, "The decorator lady is preparing me to be heaven's decorator," and, "When I'm in heaven, I'll decorate a corner just for her."

On another occasion I visited a home for unwed mothers and took some of our *Home Interiors* plaques, candles, figurines, and other pretty objects for use in the girls' rooms. I had the happy opportunity of being able to talk to the girls about what they could do to make their rooms more attractive—and as their interest and excitement grew, they became interested in improving their bedrag-

gled and unkempt physical appearance as well. Soon their behavior, their studies—every area of their life—changed for the better.

These are just a few of the many, many experiences I've had that show how important are the objects and colors that surround us. Today we live in an age of what I call "distractamania"—so many things always pulling us in different directions. That's why the idea of home is so important—whether it means a room in an institution or the place where a little boy wants to have his Scout meeting, whether it's a compact apartment or rambling house, whether one person lives there or many.

Home is a sanctuary, a place we can come to and feel "I'm loved, I'm cared for." In my mind, I think of the old-fashioned notion of a drawbridge—when you come home, you pull the drawbridge up . . . and are *safe*. And when you enter the door, it doesn't matter if it's a mansion or a cottage, whether you're rich or poor, easygoing or ambitious—all that matters is that the contents were assembled with zest and caring. And that the gathering of all these things wasn't a duty, but a privilege. As Phillips Brooks said, "Duty makes us do things well, but love makes us do them beautifully."

Whatever your situation or temperament happens to be, in the following pages you'll see an array of easy, inexpensive, appealing ideas to make your home magical. You'll get an overall view of the most promising and practical techniques and styles that will set you thinking and

"Come on in!" The door is open to a home filled with love.

Serenity is the feeling conveyed by the green and white of this charming, timeless foyer (*above right*). Making use of an often-neglected area below a staircase is not only practical, but also attractive ... due in large part here to the excellent coordination of the eclectic furnishings (*below right*).

give you a new perspective about what makes a room larger, smaller, more attractive. You'll learn about color—one of my favorite subjects!—and how it affects your emotions, how it can be used to surround you in glorious ways. And we'll shed some fascinating light on decorating language and terms and history that you can apply in your own life.

We have a Code of Ethics at *Home Interiors and Gifts*, and I'd like to share it with you here:

We believe in the dignity and importance of women—
We believe that everything woman touches should be ennobled by that touch—
We believe that the home is the greatest influence on the character of mankind—

We believe the home should be a haven . . . a place of refuge, a place of peace, a place of harmony, a place of beauty—
No home in America ever need be dull and unattractive.
We are dedicated to doing our part to make every home have Attraction Power.

So whether you want to start from scratch or simply pep up and make the most of what you've got, stand by for the news. Here are the decorating philosophies my wonderful co-workers and I have developed over the years, the absolutely fascinating knowledge and tricks of our trade that have meant the most to beloved friends and clients around the country. After all, love has a locale on earth—and it is called . . . home.

And so . . . this book is lovingly dedicated to the Homemakers of America, for you are a Homemaker whether you are single and creating a home for yourself in an apartment, a condo, a mobile home, or elsewhere. You are a Homemaker if you are a wife and creating a home for yourself and your husband, wherever it might be, and you are a Homemaker whenever you are creating a wonderful family atmosphere . . . whether it be for yourself, husband, children, parents, or others.

We want this to be a practical book that you can pick up, enjoy, and have fun with, and truly learn to decorate your home with love.

Enjoy it as you do it, because it is your home, and it must reflect your taste and your personality. We hope your home will truly be filled with lots of love for all the family members who live therein and all who enter.

MARY C. CROWLEY
CHAPEL KNOLL
DALLAS

MARY C. CROWLEY'S Decorate Your Home with Love

Little Daisies/Gigi copyright © Katzenbach & Warren, Inc.

Color–What a
Remarkable Rainbow!

Color! It's the magic ingredient that makes any home come alive, that soothes our spirits—or makes them sing. Color can make a room swing—or sparkle. It can give a room pizzazz, set off a sense of stimulation and excitement. Or it can create a homey, comfortable look that you want to snuggle up to and stay in. Color can make you feel happy and cheerful, or—if used without understanding—it can subdue you and make you feel a little dull and moody.

Color influences your life in endless, amazing ways, probably far more than you realize. Color adds excitement, gaiety, spontaneity, life. Color can be a retreat: It brings quietness, serenity, peace. The study of color is endlessly fascinating and deeply satisfying. I never get tired of learning more and more about this important and exciting field.

Oh, God could have made the world in black and white. And the soil would still have nourished potatoes, and the trees would still have borne fruit. But God knew that we'd all need color to add delight and beauty, zest and comfort to our lives. It's one of His incredibly great gifts to us—and when we use it in our homes, it's our gift to those we love . . . and to ourselves.

Because I consider color so important, I'm going to tell you everything I can about it. Hold on for a happy ride around the color carousel.

The Remarkable Rainbow Wheel

Color *is* light. We see its range reflected when drops of water act as prisms and break sunlight into glorious rainbow hues. And although an infinite number of colors can be combined in an endless number of ways, there are some combinations that work especially well together. Has it been years since you studied the primary colors in school, even colored in a "wheel" of your own? Well, let's cast a fresh and excited new eye at that color wheel—and remind ourselves just what these beautiful colors are and how they work together.

Primary colors are the heart of our wheel, the three colors from which all other colors are made. They are the dynamic triumvirate of red, yel-

low, and blue—and are color in its strongest, most elementary, and vibrant form.

Secondary colors are the three colors that result if you mix equal parts of the primary colors: green (a mix of yellow and blue); orange (a mix of red and yellow); and violet (a mix of red and blue).

Tertiary colors are the ones that occur if you mix a primary color with its nearest secondary color. Tertiary colors are blue-green, yellow-green, yellow-orange, red-orange, red-violet, and blue-violet. These colors are made of "thirds," because mixing half and half means you have two-thirds red and one-third orange, creating a red-orange.

By using these combinations, you can bring color into your life and home in a great variety of luscious ways.

Some Terms to Tempt You

Now to the ways each of the wheel's colors can be adapted to *your* needs and desires! And to explain that, I'll give you a "color vocabulary" that will apply to and help you with the colors *you* pick.

Hue is simply another word for color. Red, green, and blue? They're all hues.

Shade results when black is added to a color. Sometimes you'll hear people saying, "What a beautiful shade of pink." But that's incorrect. Midnight blue, forest green, deep purple—*those* are shades.

Tint results when white is added to a color. So *that's* what pink is. Baby blue, petal pink, buttercup yellow, whispery lavender—pastel colors are tints.

Tone is the result when equal amounts of white *and* black (a combination that actually amounts to gray) are added to a color. So red or yellow or whatever color you have is literally "toned down" by the addition, and becomes less vibrant and more subdued.

Knowing all these terms allows you to look at the color red in a new light. For starters, our gorgeous friend red is a hue. But when tinted with white, it becomes pink. When shaded with black, it becomes burgundy or maroon. When toned down with gray, it's something in between. And all up and down the scale, you have a whole range of reds to work with. And this is true for every one of the twelve colors on the color wheel. Talk about rainbows!

Now on to some other terms that are often used in decorating and that you should know.

Value refers to the lightness or darkness of a color. White is the highest or lightest value; black the lowest or darkest. A color's value— light or dark—has a lot to do with how it works in a room and the mood it creates.

Intensity refers to a color's purity, to the amount of strong natural color it still contains. Decorators also sometimes call this a color's "satura-

tion"—the vivid, vibrant hue present in any color that hasn't been toned or shaded or tinted into a more muted variation.

Happy Harmonies

Let's go back to our color wheel for some guidelines about what color groups are good friends—about how they work together and can be combined to create the look *you* like.

Complementary colors are the ones that are just opposite each other on the color wheel. Using these colors together in a room or setting can be satisfying, but you must use a bit more skill because in their basic and strongest primary form they are so vibrant that they may sometimes neutralize each other—or "knock each other out."

Here's an example. Red and green are directly opposite each other on the wheel. If put together in a room in their "pure" form, the total look of the room might end up gray, rather than the merry look of red and green that you probably hoped you'd achieve.

Here's another interesting thing about these two complementary colors. Often when I'm conducting meetings, I'll hang a square of very vibrant red on a white sheet and ask the audience to look at it intently for about sixty seconds. Then I remove the red square but ask the audience to keep their eyes on the same place. And what do they see? Green. It's a visual illustration of what is called afterimage. It's nature's way of adjusting or compensating for an excess of something, and when there is a bold,

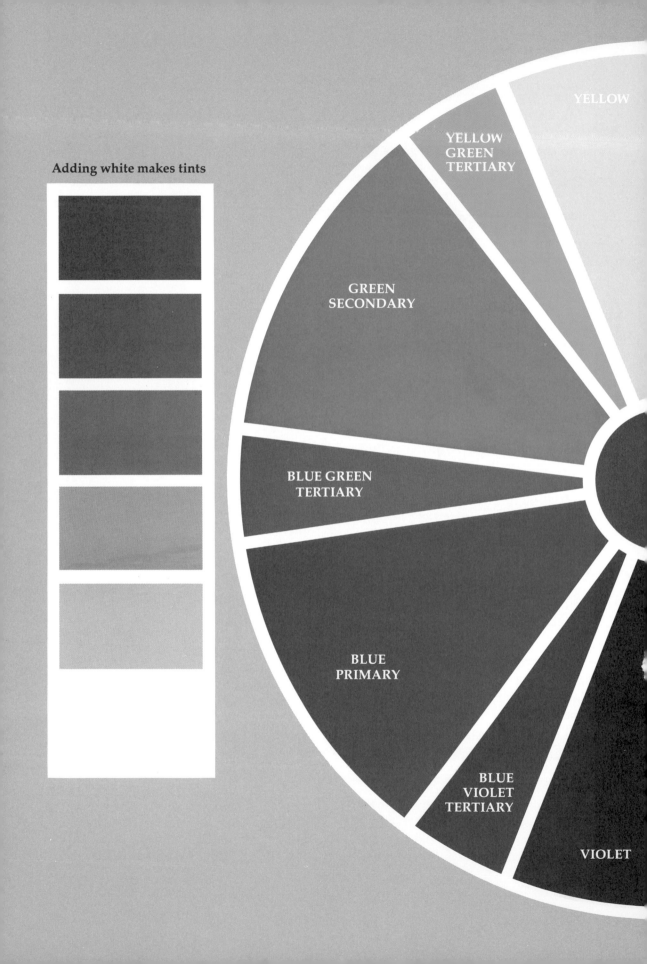

Adding white makes tints

YELLOW

YELLOW
GREEN
TERTIARY

GREEN
SECONDARY

BLUE GREEN
TERTIARY

BLUE
PRIMARY

BLUE
VIOLET
TERTIARY

VIOLET

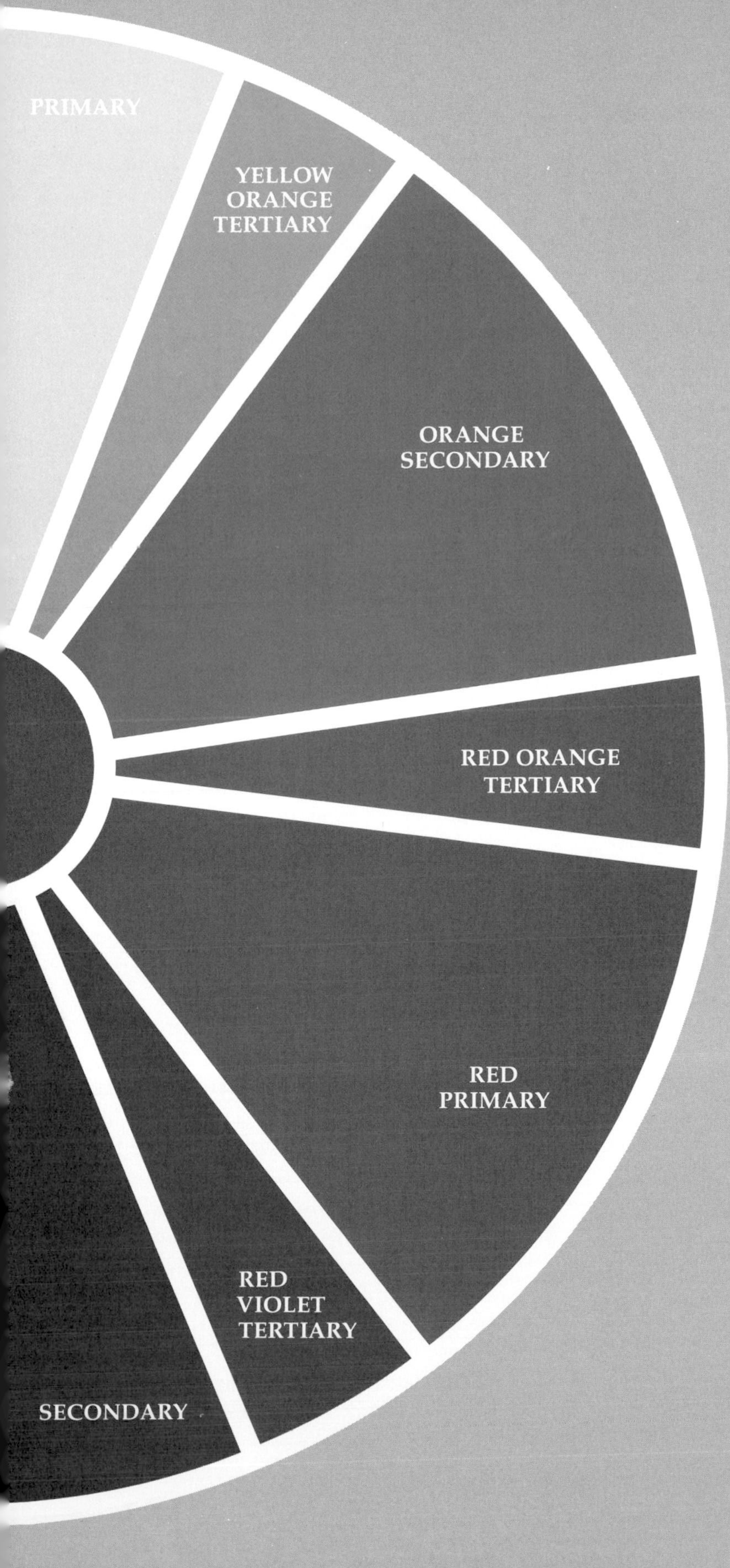

PRIMARY

YELLOW
ORANGE
TERTIARY

ORANGE
SECONDARY

RED ORANGE
TERTIARY

RED
PRIMARY

RED
VIOLET
TERTIARY

SECONDARY

Adding black makes shades

hot color coming at your eye for any length of time, nature immediately compensates at its removal by giving you an afterimage of a cooler, softer color.

As far as fashion is concerned, if you are wearing a bright red blouse and gray slacks, a person gazing at your blouse and then your slacks will see an afterimage of green on the slacks. The color will be different from what you thought—and hoped —was being seen. If you wear a green blouse and brown slacks, the after-image on the slacks will be red, which will completely change the color of the brown. So that's why you need to proceed with caution when using complementary colors. You may not be creating the illusion you think you are.

However, when you use tints and tones and shades of red and green, it's a different story! Red can be used as sunset pink, or dreamy rose, or a robust wine color; green might be misty sea foam green, or inviting avocado, or nestle-up-against-me moss green. Just imagine how beautifully *these* combinations of red and green go together. So it's clear that you *can* create an effective and enormously appealing color scheme by using . . . complementary colors.

Split complementary colors means you're slipping directly next door on the color wheel and using not just the complementary colors but also those tertiary colors next to them. Let's use red and green as an example again: Here's red—and now, moving opposite to green, we'll also use the yellow-green and blue-green that are alongside. When you examine pictures of rooms that are pleasing in magazines or books, you'll see that many use split-complementary color schemes—they're very popular and open up any number of possible harmonies to you.

Analogous colors are those *not* opposite, but *side by side*, on the color wheel—colors that are adjacent to each other. This means you're taking your secondary and tertiary colors and using them—often with the primary color they're right next to— in a blend that's especially appealing. Just think of blue and the colors analogous (or adjacent) to it—blue, blue-green, blue-violet, and violet— and you'll see what I mean. Or for sunnier possibilities, imagine red-orange, orange, yellow-orange, yellow, yellow-green, and the tints and shades of all those.

I do have to give you a word of caution about using these colors. Side-by-side colors on the wheel can be simply delightful—as long as you don't "wheel" too far and get into the head of the next color "family."

Think of it this way: The three primary colors are heads of families, and the secondary and tertiary colors are the kids and the cousins. The kids and the cousins who are side by side can be used together, and also with that one "head-of-the-family" the kids and cousins gather around. But you cannot break out of this cozy family setting and pull in another family head—then a real ruckus starts.

Some years ago a major airline decided to break all the rules of color harmony and redo the interiors as well as the outsides of their planes in splashes and splops (I know that's not a real word but it should be) of purple and red and orange and *everything*, whether the colors went together or not. Well, this jumble of colors created a lot of publicity all right, but it also got passengers and airport onlookers jangled. And *those* folks didn't complain nearly as much as the flight attendants and people who actually worked on and around the airplanes did. The airline executives had so many complaints that they finally had to tone things down and make the colors more harmonious. So remember: Blue and its cousins blue-green and blue-purple are pleasing indeed. But drag in primary red in full force, and you'll have a jarring mess.

Monochromatic colors—*one* color used in its many ranges and possibilities—are seen in many homes today. So you love blue? Well, use it and only it in a variety of tints and shades, from soft sky blue to robust navy.

I'm going to stop right here and mention—

Accent colors. Accent colors are splashes of color that "punctuate" the basic color scheme you've carried out in walls and rugs and furniture. Accent colors can be added in accessories—in a pillow or throw rug, vase or figurine, candle or footstool. And especially in a monochromatic color scheme, an accent of another color is important.

If using blue, you might reach right across your color wheel and use or-

ange as an accent color. Or red or yellow—in its most vibrant hue, or perhaps in a tint or shade, depending on the monochromatic range you've chosen. It's fun to choose and use accent colors—in pillows or throw rugs or any of the wonderful range of accessories we'll be talking about in a later chapter.

Triad colors are popular nowadays, too. These are sometimes called "flag colors" because they're the kind so boldly used on actual flags. America's own red, white, and blue is an example of this (more about white in just a minute). Red, blue, and yellow would be another effective triad. So would violet, green, and orange. Any three colors that are an equal distance from each other on the color wheel constitute a triad—or any two such colors used with, say, white or black.

Some Wondrous Ways With White and Black

Over the years *white* has sometimes been defined as "the absence of all colors" and *black* as "the combination of all colors." Well, that definition doesn't suit me at all, because to me it's just the opposite. In a room flooded with sunlight, if you look into the sunlight long enough, it almost becomes white, doesn't it? And if you take a crystal prism and hang it in the window, that "white light" will separate into beautiful rainbow hues. At the same time, if there's no light at all, there's blackness. So for me white is the presence of *all* colors and light; black is the absence of those things.

White is the magic ingredient that unifies and brightens this living room. And black is the important exclamation point!

Oriental Vine®, Duval®, Porcelain Border®, Hillham, copyright Greeff Fabrics, Inc.

Romantically feminine, the mood of this room is achieved through the harmonious use of fabrics and wall-coverings in tints and shades of complementary colors. Flowers lend their charm.

This bedroom retreat provides an atmosphere of relaxation through its monochromatic color scheme. The variety of textures and materials is important in any such scheme.

Children love bold colors and this workable bedroom makes striking use of the patriotic triad colors of red, white, and blue. The use of split-bamboo blinds grants a degree of privacy.

White is a magic ingredient in any room setting. Whether you're start-ing your decorating from scratch or giving a lift to an already-existing decor, white is the "color" that unites, lifts, harmonizes. I think we've all gone into homes that seemed a chaos of color, a little of this, a whoosh of that. Well, here's the magic trick I learned from other experts: In decorating, use white in a way that is extensive and important enough to gather all other colors to-gether, creating harmony out of a chaotic atmosphere.

Here's an example of what I mean. I once visited a woman whose living room was a real hodgepodge of colors. My nerves start to jangle just thinking about it. I found for her a low wicker table that I sprayed white, put into the room as a coffee table, and placed on it an all-white flower arrangement. Then I sprayed some wall sconces white and hung them above the sofa. It was amazing how the white gathered everything to-gether, how your eye was drawn to this attractive grouping. The white created a peaceful, orderly serenity in that room of many colors.

Another woman asked my help in improving the decor in her husband's restaurant. The walls were paneled in dark, wine-colored leather, and the atmosphere was oppressive to say the least. "I can't afford to completely re-decorate and change the upholstery," the owner said. "Is there *anything* I can do?"

White to the rescue again! The room contained four huge redwood tubs that had once housed live plants. We painted those tubs several coats of sparkling bright white and rein-stated new greenery. The transfor-mation was immediate! That impor-tant statement of white lightened everything in the room and created a cheerful atmosphere.

This "White Is Always Right" phi-losophy can be translated into any room or situation in your own life. If you're dying to "do something" but your money and time are limited, buy some white paint or accessories or fabric and make magic. White plus any one other color—or combi-nation of colors—is an absolutely foolproof color scheme.

Just as white unifies and brightens, black is the exclamation point, that little something that brings the rest into focus. Just look at the human face—varying tones of skin and hair all "brought together" by that little jet-black pupil in the center of the eye. Sometimes in a wash of white, that touch of black will be just what you need—in a candleholder or pil-low or vase or end table.

This isn't to say that you can't do the reverse and use black as a basic part of your room color scheme— and allow white to provide the excla-mation point. If your room contains wrought iron or mahogany or simply an abundance of more somber colors, then it's the white that will act as that "pupil of the eye" for you and pro-vide that "zing!" of a focal point you need.

The Go-With-Everything Neutrals

I can't leave this subject without talking about the neutrals—the grays, browns, and beiges that are so easy on the eyes and soothing to the soul that it's no wonder so many people choose them for their homes. Colors of wheat and champagne and putty and oatmeal indeed often go with everything and are good choices for long-term enjoyment.

But there are some cautions, particularly if you're using gray. True gray is an equal mixture of black and white. But if you take equal parts of any two colors directly opposite on the color wheel, you'll have gray as well. Equal parts of red and green? Gray. Blue-purple and yellow-orange? They equal gray, too.

It's important to keep this in mind if gray is an integral part of your color scheme. Have you ever tried to match a scarf or blouse or purse with a gray suit? You may have thought, "Oh, blue will surely go with that," only to discover when putting them side by side that it doesn't at all. This is because your suit wasn't a true gray, but a combination of red and green, or two other colors that weren't complementary to blue.

This is why gray is so difficult to use in decorating or fashion—you have to know the component parts of that particular gray, or test just how items look together by experimenting with swatches or samples or color charts.

Now that I've swirled you around this wondrous carousel of colors, it's time to look at how these colors can make magic for *you*. Hold on, the fun is just beginning!

Make Your Own

Color Magic!

2

In a way, it's like being a magician. But instead of pulling rabbits out of your hat, you're pulling bouquets of color—color that tricks others (in the nicest possible way) into thinking rooms are smaller, larger, lighter, more elegant or up-to-date than they actually are.

Much of this illusion is created by the "warmth" or the "coolness" of a color. The "warms" are the sunshine colors of red, yellow, and orange, and they're actually the color beams that reach our eyes most immediately and perk us up most quickly. The "cools" are the deep and dreamy colors of sea and woods and grassy fields—blue and green and purple; these colors come to our eyes in a more leisurely fashion and create an illusion of depth and repose. (In fact, if you put a thermometer into a bucket of paint, you'd discover that the warm colors are literally a higher temperature than the cool ones!)

It all works together so perfectly; our good God knew what He was about when He created the world. A noted color expert once asked me to think about what would happen if one morning we all woke up and the sky were orange and the grass were red. He pointed out that we wouldn't need any bomb to destroy ourselves—the emotional impact of these color changes would be so devastating that we'd all simply go berserk. But God *knew* what miracle array of colors was right for His children. Blue sky, green grass, rich brown earth, golden sun—what could be more . . . *right?*

When we bring these blessed colors into our own homes, they affect us in fascinating ways. Here's an amazing example: A color laboratory in New York set up a dining room in which everything—walls, furniture, tablecloths—was entirely white. In the ceiling, however, was a huge light and color wheel that could be revolved to color the room in various hues.

A number of people were invited to lunch, and when they arrived, the room was awash in a soft yellow-orange, a color that's very conducive to good dining. Well, the meal was going along just fine, when, unknown to the guests, the color engineer turned the overhead color wheel to chartreuse! Four people actually became ill, others simply pushed their plates aside; conversation died down,

and a depressing pall settled over the room. After ten minutes of this, the color engineer switched back to the apricot color. Conversation picked up, people reached for their plates and started to eat again. The guests left that meal never realizing what an impact color had had on their emotional behavior and on their very appetites!

That's how important color is. Whether or not you're intellectually aware of the colors that surround you, your subconscious *is* responding. Certain colors are known to have certain effects on the nervous system. Red, for instance, revs you up. If you have a bright red kitchen, I can almost promise you your kids will battle and squirm and carry on through breakfast, lunch, and dinner. I visited with a woman whose kitchen walls, the ones surrounding the family's meal area, were fire-engine red. I asked her if her little boys fought a lot at mealtime. "How did you know?" she asked, astonished. I explained that a color like that can set off anybody's adrenaline, and suggested that even if she couldn't repaint the walls by the next meal, she could at least change the bright red tablecloth. She not only did that, but in a few weeks she called to say she'd wallpapered over those dazzling walls with a cheery but subdued yellow pattern. "Things have really settled down," she told me. "Now we can eat in peace."

And please don't paint a bedroom red either. I consulted with one woman whose bedroom was done in so much Chinese red that my eyes hurt just looking at it. "Honey, if you and your husband wake up to this, you're really starting out on the wrong foot," I told her. I can't help but think that repainting her bedroom a soothing blue saved her marriage.

The reds and dazzling oranges and "hot" pinks and other related colors that I call "Yippee!" colors should go into the playroom or den or recreation areas, where you *want* to stimulate activity. Do you know that some restaurants *purposely* use red on their walls and in their decor in order to "move" customers. They don't want people settling in and relaxing, they want them to eat and run, so they can pack in even more people.

Let's go back to that apricot for a moment. Orange, yellow, and yellow-orange are the colors known to arouse our appetites. I know of a man so severely depressed that he refused to eat for days and finally was hospitalized. Fortunately his good friend happened to be a doctor who had worked extensively with color, and who asked that his friend's hospital room be painted orange. The depressed man was in such serious condition that the staff even ended up dyeing the sheets orange, making everything in the room orange. It wasn't long before the patient had snapped out of it and was ravenous and asking for food. The downward pull of his depression had been overcome by the upward pull of that orange.

What about the other colors? Well, each of them exerts an effect and your preference says something about your personality. Here are some general observations that may

or may not hold true for you—but in any event, it's fun to consider them.

Green? Green is comforting. If you love green, you're a good neighbor, reliable, probably a member of local clubs or groups. You have a balanced relationship with others, are stable and friendly, and can be counted on.

Yellow is for intellectuals. If you love yellow, you have imagination and lofty dreams. You love contemporary furnishings and objects. And, since yellow is clearly such a sunny color, people who love it usually have sunny dispositions.

Blue is soothing—and since everyone likes to be soothed, it's a color you can count on to succeed in just about every setting. Blue is also for conservatives. If you love blue, you're deliberate, sensitive, and conscientious.

Pink is gentle; even men who fuss about it are secretly at home in rooms of this color (but don't force it on them, it's part of their image to insist they like "manly" blues or greens). If you love pink, you're partial to the finer things in life—and are probably a satisfied soul, quiet and ladylike.

Orange is cheery—and as we noted before, is very likely to stimulate your appetite. Orange lovers are sociable, get along with people easily, but *are* concerned about whether people reciprocate and like them back.

Purple? Well, hmmm, I have to say that if you like purple, you're probably a bit temperamental. To some people's way of thinking, purple in large quantities is considered depressing and unbalancing. In fact,

Sweet Williams/French Ribbon Border copyright © Katzenbach & Warren, Inc.

Yellow is truly a sunny color. Here, in
this contemporary look, is an excellent
example of the mood it conveys.

Monelle/Monelle Border/Tansy/Gigi copyright © Katzenbach & Warren, Inc.

A more traditional look is achieved in this setting with the delicate print accented by a gentle shade of rose. Note the artful use of accessories.

there's a theory that some of the royal heads of Europe were unbalanced because they were surrounded by so much purple! Whether this is true or not, I think a little purple goes a long way—and should be used for special accents rather than great expanses of walls and rugs.

Brown is earthy. If it's one of your favorites, you're likely to be dependable, practical, thrifty, hardworking, and devoted to your family. But remember that brown is one of those "mixture" colors like gray that may be made up of a variety of other colors: It might be a combination of orange and yellow-orange and red-orange; it might be a combo of yellow, yellow-green, and red-orange. There are so many variations of brown, according to its component parts, that you almost always have to check it with swatches or samples to make sure it fits into your particular scheme and setting.

Speaking of gray, *gray* is cautious. If this is your color, you like comfort more than glamor. You're clinical and neat rather than fashionable—and considering what's "in fashion" one minute (and out the next), I say that's just fine. In the final analysis, it's always important to go with what you and your family like, and not be swayed by some popular style that doesn't suit you at all!

Black is worldly. If you love black, you're sophisticated, clever, and do things somewhat out of the ordinary. You're chic and contemporary and unpredictable. But frankly, you could use a little color in your life.

Of course, as our moods change, so do our preferences for color. So this little color run-through was mostly just for fun. But I hope it's started you thinking about how important the use of color is in your life. It's a real mood maker and the most important element to consider when you start to decorate.

But now back to business and some more basics you should consider when choosing colors for your home.

Texture makes a big difference in how colors will actually appear. The exact same shade will look different depending on whether it's done up in satin or velvet or shag. Just think of a blue seersucker suit that looks so cool and pleasant. Imagine that same color blue as it would look in a satin suit, or a nubby wool suit. It's a totally different look and image.

Texture adds a lot to any room. Shag rugs, corduroy slipcovers, burlap used for wall coverings or to serve as a backdrop for sconces or mirrors, materials that are tufted or woven—all make a room more interesting and appealing. In the eighties, we've been subjected to a lot of "high tech" furnishings—chrome and steel and plastic furniture and architecture, all sorts of rough and metallic accessories. But who can really feel at home in all this hard-edged gleam and shivery glitz? It gives *me* a shudder just thinking about it.

It's clear why the textures you use are important, both for the look *and* the feel. When choosing things for your home, run your hands over them. These are items your family will be sitting on, snuggling against, using as armrests or pillows or rest-

Structural details are decorative factors
in their own right as can be seen in the
wood carving on the staircase and unusual window.

The white walls in this room make for a feeling of spaciousness and highlight the dark natural wood beams and fireplace molding (*above*). Providing a subtle backdrop for the vibrant triad colors in the pillows are the neutral tones of the carpeting, walls, and upholstered pieces. A change in mood can easily be achieved by a change in fabric (*above right*). The complementary colors in the fabric of the upholstered pieces are a fine foil for the accessories in this eclectic living room (*below right*).

ing places. You want them to feel *good*. But again I caution you to remember that the color you use will change according to the texture you choose to go with it. The exact same color of avocado will look one way in a shag rug and utterly another on a piece of velvet. And that satin cushion dyed to "exactly match" that velour sofa will instead look much brighter and lighter.

Finish is the physical surface on certain items, and it too affects a color's "color." Exactly the same color used on a lacquered chest or Parsons table will look quite different on an old wicker chest, or a wall that's stucco, or one that's smooth and flat.

Space and size affect color. A bit of turquoise or a dash of magenta may look fetching on a small scale, but beware of covering an entire wall with either one. Again and again people will pick out a sample at the paint store that looks charming when it's the size of a postage stamp—but is overwhelming when applied to bigger areas or an entire wall.

Opening things up. You can do it with lighter colors. If a room or area is cramped or dingy, light colors will "lift" the ceilings and "spread wide" the walls. And if you're dealing with an area that's broken up into nooks and eaves and crannies and entryways, a light color will help blend things all together into an airy whole. If your room has few windows or doesn't receive much sunlight, light colors not only brighten the mood

but enhance the natural light available and create an illusion—there's that magic word again—of all possible light.

Making things more snug. Sometimes you have the opposite problem and a room is simply too vast. Then dark colors can be used to make a "white elephant" of a room seem intimate and cozy—or if high walls soar *too* much, paint the ceiling in a dark color to achieve a warmer, more comforting look.

Squaring things up. If you have a skinny hallway or funny little narrow room, you can make things seem more square and spacious by painting smaller, shorter walls in darker colors, and longer and narrower walls in lighter colors. This contrast in colors will make things seem more in proportion.

Emphasizing the positive. Use this same contrasting-colors technique to play up details in your home that deserve attention. Painting or staining wainscoting, moldings, railings, banisters, and overhead beams in a color that contrasts with adjoining walls or floors creates an attractive effect. And marvelous details that would otherwise be lost are highlighted.

Clever camouflage. Swinging to the opposite situation, sometimes there are features in your home that you want to play down rather than up. You might have a wall broken up by too many doors, or a strange little window frame over a dumpy-looking radiator. Whatever these odds and ends are, you can do a vanishing act and cover them all—walls and frames and doors and everything—in the same color.

Simple lifesaving. We've all looked at that old chest of drawers or bookcase, even at an entire room, and thought it was hopeless. And how many pieces of furniture languish in cellar or attic simply because they seem so dreary we can't bear to have them around. But a can of paint is like a magic wand, transforming "ugly duckling" odds and ends into charming swans. Smooth on a bright new coat of paint (you could even make it a family project and ask the kids to help), buy some snazzy new drawer pulls or knobs from the hardware store, and top things off with some charming accessories (more about that in a later chapter). Presto chango! Color's made a new piece of furniture, a new look, a new room!

Now that you've got all these magic tricks up your sleeve, you can turn to them whenever you want them. Spin your own magic spell!

My favorite kind of kitchen is one that blends or flows into an even larger room, and here I am in mine. I love to cook, and I treasure the "Best Cook Award" given me some time ago. It's my belief that home is the kitchen test of the Gospel, and on the cabinets behind me are three verses from Scripture that are a constant source of comfort and challenge to me. They, along with the fruits and flowers above them, were hand painted by a dear friend and serve to remind me:

This is the day which the Lord hath made; let us rejoice and be glad in it.
Psalms 118:24

Delight Thyself also in the Lord; and he shall give thee the desires of thine heart.
Psalms 37:4

Trust in the Lord with all thine heart; and lean not unto thine own understanding.
Proverbs 3:5

The Heart of the Home— The Kitchen

3

Home is truly where the heart is. And I'm going to take that one step further and say that the heart of that heart is the kitchen. Much of my young life was spent on a farm, where I helped my grandmother in the spacious kitchen, cooking for both family members and the friendly threshing crews that my grandfather employed. The kitchen had a big, round table covered by a cheerful, checkered cloth, and some of my fondest memories are of people gathered around it, talking and dreaming and sharing ideas. That round table seemed to me like the hub of a huge wheel at the very center of the rambling house and busy home. Just thinking about it, I want to give that kitchen table a hug.

I guess I've never gotten over those early feelings, because I still love a big kitchen—and a big round table. And I still want it—and me—to be at the hub of activity. My favorite kind of kitchen is one that blends or flows into an even larger room, so there's a whole lot of living incorporated into this one important area. My own kitchen isn't separated by any walls from my living room; everything just meshes together into one large, enveloping room. When I'm cooking, creating, preparing exciting things for family or friends, I'm still right in the middle of activity, where everything is going on. It makes everything so much merrier!

At my grandmother's kitchen table so much went on. In those early years we didn't have electricity, so in the evening my grandmother would light the old-fashioned oil lamp that was at the center of the table. It was by that flickering light that I studied my first-grade books. Grandfather would sit there, too, reading his paper, and Grandmother would talk with me or darn socks in the golden glow. Oh, I'm sure all of you have your own beautiful memories! Perhaps not of the days before electricity—but each in your own way must remember some of the wondrous moments and smells and sounds of the kitchens of your childhood.

But whatever your memories of the past, I hope that now you're planning to *make* memories for those who gather around your own kitchen table. I hope that as you too plan and prepare to meet the needs of your friends and family you'll make sure your own kitchen has a place for read-

ing, talking, studying, sharing. So many modern kitchens today are quite compact, and in many apartment kitchens space is truly at a minimum.

I was in a New York City apartment kitchen recently, and there was barely space for two people to pass each other, much less room for a whole threshing crew to sit down! But regardless of how cramped our living quarters become, I think that most homes in America will indeed always have at least *some* space for family members to snack, or have a quick breakfast or cup of steaming soup or hot chocolate. No matter how compact the spaces are we live in, or how on-the-run are the lives we lead, that settle-down-for-a-minute spot in the kitchen will always mean a lot to us. And will always deserve the best decorating touches you can give it.

Small or large, make sure your kitchen is a "center place." Try to design or rearrange the decor so that you—and everyone else—have enough room to move around in, and so that whoever is preparing the meals can move easily and efficiently from refrigerator to stove, from work area to serving table. If you're lucky enough to be designing a kitchen from scratch, this is the place to make sure (perhaps more than any other room in the house) that the doors of stove and refrigerator have ample room to open without bringing other activity in the kitchen to a dead stop, that drawers can pull out easily without causing a traffic jam.

There are so many appliances today that make everybody's life so much easier—and allow us to spend more time with our family and friends, and more time working on creative projects both inside and outside the home that interest us and help others. My favorite new "invention" is the microwave oven; I think it's a real time and energy saver. I'd suggest making room for one (unless, of course, you have someone with a heart pacemaker in your family) even if you have to put it on top of the refrigerator or suspend it in or under one of your cabinets, because it is certainly "worth its space." Especially for busy families that are always coming and going, it's a real convenience to pop something in the microwave and have it hot and bubbling just minutes later.

Oh, a kitchen should be an inviting place. It should invite those coming home late from work or a date or a class or club meeting to "sit down, have a glass of milk and some cookies or fruit—and talk over what happened that evening or reminisce about occurrences of the past." It should invite early birds up at the crack of dawn to start the day with a steaming cup of coffee or tea, and look ahead to what the day will hold. It should invite a neighbor in for cinnamon toast, or carolers in for cider and doughnuts, or out-of-town guests in for a holiday feast.

The decorations, the accessories you include all "add up to" this invitation. And the touches you assemble are all your own. Many people love the fresh and attractive look of blue and white china (you see it on page 47), others want gay plastic dishes for rough-and-tumble everyday. A fresh, bright tablecloth can make a world of difference, so can cheery cloth napkins (and you don't need to groan at the thought of the ironing, today there are many synthetic fabrics that wash clean as a whistle in the washing machine and then can go from a tumble in the dryer right onto the table).

Many people today love the look of a country kitchen—and I'm among them. It's a real delight to develop a room with exposed brick walls, glowing wood cabinetry, antique finishes and rustic details, all set off by calico or patchwork prints in wallpaper, curtains, seat cushions. And always, of course, it's delightful to add a rosy geranium in the window, or a pot of ivy or a little bouquet of silk flowers. And don't forget a place for a candle. There's nothing more exciting than having a late-night snack by candlelight.

I realize we live in a fast-paced world. But somehow I think we *have* to have in our kitchens, in the places where we eat, some of the graces and civilized touches that get us through our busy days. We *need* the charm of fabric and color and texture. Yes, we have to have surfaces that are smooth and functional and are easily cleaned in our refrigerators and stoves, and on our counter tops. But in addition, in the place where we sit and take a moment to share the details of our day over a buttery croissant or fragrant cup of soup, let us also add something that is of beauty and texture and feeds our souls. If you have a very white kitchen, you need to bring in accent colors and warm personalizing touches to keep the room

Brick, tile, and wood combine to set the scene for this dramatic yet inviting dining-kitchen. Bright flowers and brilliant color enliven the compact, well-designed work area (*left*). The center island does double duty as a functional working surface and beautifully appointed buffet table (*center*). The accessories, from flowers to suspended garlic braid, to copper pots hung from overhead racks, contribute significantly to the decor. The Mexican motif is carried out in the table setting (*right*). How warm and welcoming! And how well decorated "with love."

from becoming harsh and cold. You can do this with colors, with textures, you can do it with flowers or pottery or copper pans hung bright and gleaming from wall hooks or an overhead rack. Chintz cushions on the stools of an eating counter invite the most agitated eaters to relax and stay awhile.

Place mats are another way to add bright touches of color. (Fingertip terry towels come in a myriad of colors and can be put to use as practical place mats.) You can even tack straw place mats to the wall, then add a picture or plaque or sconce in its center to make a textured and charming wall hanging. Baskets go wonderfully on kitchen walls, too—either flat with their woven backs showing, or attached perpendicularly to the wall in such a way that they can hold recipes, phone messages, odds and ends.

Baskets and bowls of fruits and nuts make delightful (and nutritious) centerpieces. I love to cook with wooden spoons (having those around is another touch of homey texture), and I keep mine in an attractive pitcher—it's another way of adding your own personal touch to your kitchen.

It's important to have "inspiration" in any room in which you spend a lot of time. This is certainly true in the kitchen! On the wooden cabinet doors in my kitchen have been painted some Bible verses that mean a great deal to me and that have kept me calm and cheerful through many a hectic day. "This is the day the Lord hath made, let us rejoice and be glad in it—Psalms 118:24" is painted

just about at eye level on one cabinet. This just reminds me that every day is a gift from God, that He has made this day. And it's full of duties, responsibilities, disappointments, challenges—but it's also full of wonder, and of joyful opportunities, it's full of potential for rich friendships and service to others, and the making of whole brand-new memories.

On another cabinet, just across from my telephone that rings all too frequently, are these words: "Let the words of my mouth and the meditations of my heart be acceptable in Thy sight, O Lord—Psalms 19:14." I constantly have to be reminded of this, especially when that phone rings when I'm in the middle of cooking dinner! Fortunately I have a long cord on my phone, and can continue cooking while I talk—and today they have those new cordless phones that are a help to so many homemakers. But the biggest help of all is that Bible verse, believe me.

I've heard it said that "home is the kitchen test of the Gospel." If the Gospel message doesn't work in our homes, how can we make it work in the world? In our homes we're *truly* ourselves and sometimes take off the best-behavior masks we wear in public. It is in our homes that the people we live with see us as we really are. This realization has swept over me many a time, and I have had to renew my determination to make the Gospel work in *my* home with *my* loved ones.

Back to one of my favorite subjects—color. Do you remember what we talked about in chapter two, about how color actually affects our taste buds and our very attitudes when we're eating? As you'll recall, soft oranges or yellows or peaches are colors that arouse your appetite without overstimulating your system—so these colors alone or mingled in with others are good choices for any kitchen. Especially if you have a kitchen full of metal or formica, break up that sterile look by adding cushions or wallpaper in tints of apricot, lemon, or blush pink. (If you have paneled cabinet doors, cover the recessed center with fabric in these colors.)

Sharing food—breaking bread together. It's one of the greatest opportunities for fellowship and hospitality that we have in life. Because I love cooking, and have such satisfying times in *my* kitchen, I want you to have that joy, too.

I realize that not everyone enjoys cooking—but since it has to be done, we might as well learn to love it. As Marabel Morgan put it so well in her *Total Woman Cookbook:* "I believe that creating in the kitchen is just as an authentic form of self-expression as art or music or science. My kitchen is no longer a new world to be conquered, it's my favorite room: my laboratory where I experiment; my studio where I create. I believe I'm building healthy bodies and happy memories. I am refueling not only tummies, but also hearts." And when you have decorated your kitchen so that it is a place of joy and beauty and charm, of warmth and laughter, then you'll *want* to be in that room, and you'll *want* to cook there . . . and before you know it, you *will* be loving it. Isn't it amazing how it all fits together?

But it isn't just the colors and textures and foods that say, "This kitchen is a place of love." It's also the smells! It's the wonderful aroma of freshly baked bread or heated-to-buttery-perfection croissants, of cinnamon toast tucked under the broiler, or a pot roast bubbling away in juices that fill the whole house with fragrant flavor. There's an old saying that "hunger is the best sauce" for any dish—and a sure way to arouse everyone's appetite is to fill the house with mouth watering aromas that can't be resisted. And when everyone enjoys the meals so heartily, even "cooks who don't like to cook" somehow find themselves . . . loving it!

One of my top salesladies says she always has "somethin' lovin' from the oven" when people come in the door. My own favorite "recipe for lovin' " is one I make often, usually just before guests arrive so its fragrance permeates the house. "What *is* that wonderful smell?" they say— and promptly head right for the kitchen, which suits me just fine. Here's the quick and easy **Peach Cobbler** I cook up, and then just wait to start sniffing:

Take a pan about 9" by 13" and melt a stick of butter (a quarter-pound) in the bottom. Then take four medium cans of canned peaches, and dump them juice and all into the pan. Then take a package of Duncan Hines yellow-cake mix (I get nothing out of this, I'm not advertising for them, but it does seem to work the best) and

The mellow finish of the cabinets and molding combines with the hand-decorated tiles to give warmth to this compact and efficient working area and also coordinates with the vaulted ceiling of the adjoining eating area.

Comfortable, functional, and clean of
line, this living room with dining area
typifies the contemporary look—with a
touch of country.

sprinkle it over the peaches and juice. Spread the mix and pat it down gently, then make a few holes with a fork so the juice can ooze up to the top. Melt another quarter-pound stick of butter, and dribble it over the top of the cake mix. Add a dash of nutmeg, and bake for about 45 minutes at 350 degrees.

Now if everybody is on a diet, or watching his or her cholesterol, you'd have to use something else to make a marvelous fragrance—I've heard of just sprinkling sugar and cinnamon in a pie tin and heating that to create a lovely smell. But as far as smells are concerned, I still prefer my delectable cobbler. So if you're counting calories, cook the cobbler anyway, enjoy the fragrant aroma, and give the cobbler to the neighborhood kids.

To me, "decorating with love" also includes the meals you prepare—and the fun and flair with which you prepare them. Any attractive and exciting tricks you use to make meals more pleasant and dishes more delectable will become "memory makers" for your friends and family. When my children were growing up, we didn't have much money—or television or tape decks or any of the other things that fill our homes today. We had to think of novel ways to entertain and to add excitement to our meals. So we'd soak sugar cubes in lemon extract, put them on top of scoops of ice cream in pretty glass dishes . . . and then turn out the lights! Then we'd light the sugar cubes. (The extract has a lot of alcohol in it which burns right off; I used lemon because it didn't discolor the sugar cubes.)

As the blue-tinged flames danced in the darkness, we'd all "ooh and ah." And when the tiny fire died down, the kids would say, "Oh, let's light it again, Momma!" And we'd soak the cubes again, and light them again, and "ooh and ah" all over again—it was like a bit of magic at the end of a busy day. It was fun, it was exciting, and it added a little flair in a very inexpensive way.

Here's another easy way to add flair—and make guests and family feel adored and wanted. I've talked about the pleasure of having conversation—or just plain sitting together quietly and caring—over coffee. Well, with coffee or cocoa I always bring out little containers, holding cinnamon, brown sugar, little strips of lemon or orange peel, tiny chocolate bits, nutmeg. Then each person can add exactly what pleases them. It's also wonderful to have a bowl of whipped cream to add to the flavor and fun. And if you're serving summer-frosty glasses of iced tea, it's delightful to have sprigs of garden-grown mint on hand dusted with a silvery glow of powdered sugar.

Do you think I'm getting off the subject of interior decorating? Not at all! For one thing, all the meals and "breaks" that go on in our homes are certainly "interior"—and help to decorate the whole atmosphere of the home with love. Then, too, to prepare and enjoy the food and drinks I mention here, we *use* accessories that make our kitchens so pretty.

For example, take the teapot. And tea cozy. And all the pretty cups and sugar bowls and serving trays that look so appealing sitting around our kitchens. These attractive accessories are part of a time-honored ritual that I wish more of us observed. Next to water, tea is the world's most popular drink—with a tradition stretching back for centuries. I think the English custom of stopping around three or three-thirty in the afternoon for tea is a marvelous one. It's an incredible and restoring respite to take time out of a busy day to have a cup of steaming tea and a scone or muffin with thick, clotted cream.

Years ago, when our *Home Interiors* business was young and we were seeking suppliers around the world, it was my privilege to go to the Peerage Brass Factory in Birmingham, England. What a delight it was when, in the midst of our tour of the plant, all activity ceased. We were ushered into the manager's office, someone appeared with a beautiful silver tea service, and we were all served refreshing cups of hot tea with milk or lemon.

A short time later, as we walked through the factory, we saw all the workers seated at their workbenches or around a long table with their mugs of steaming hot tea. Everything had come to a halt for the afternoon tea break. Somehow it spoke of the continuity through the years of a treasured tradition—for a time of refreshment and renewal. We all need traditions that calm us during the busy day. Whether it's a break for tea, or coffee, or milk . . . or cookies!

Everybody loves cookies—and if you have children of your own or neighborhood children nearby, I recommend that you bake often. We'll talk about centerpieces in other chapters: A pretty platter full of cookies makes a marvelous centerpiece (at least for as long as it lasts, which probably won't be long). Simple cookies are often the best, filling the house with smells of sugar and spice and everything nice as they bake. But on holidays and special occasions invite young friends in to decorate gingerbread or sugar cookies, or assemble a gingerbread house or cookie creche.

Array cookies on a bright dish or in a cheery napkin in a basket; add a sprinkling of blossoms in the spring, colored leaves in the fall, nuts and berries and fruit in the winter. But enjoy your artistic creation while you can because it's not likely to be around for long.

If you don't have a tradition of your own for family and friends, start one. Teatime, coffee break, after-school or after-work milk and cookies, time out for juice—take time to relax a minute. Count your blessings. Tell someone you love them.

The *size* of your kitchen doesn't matter a bit. Or the "circumstances" of the people using it. We live in a day when many women are working outside the home as well as in it; and many men are now sharing household duties. And more and more people of all ages are living alone, enjoying their own kitchens and yet entertaining their "extended families" in them as well. Today some families or individuals are doubling

The baker's rack serves as a showcase
for favorite items that personalize the
dining area of this modern kitchen.
Flowers and greenery make a special
contribution, as does the interesting
ceiling fixture.

Focal point in this kitchen is the artwork of the hand-painted tiles. The
bleached wood of the cabinets and the
butcher block provide a neutral background for the ceramic and copper accessories.

up and sharing living quarters; sometimes one family member cooks, sometimes two—sometimes everybody wants to get in on the act.

If your kitchen's big enough, try to arrange areas where each person can carry out her or his own culinary creations—and yet be close enough to share conversation without getting in the others' way. Some kitchens only have room for one cook at a time, some are larger and can accommodate a lot of different cooks without spoiling the broth. The kitchens you see in this chapter cover a range of situations. One is small and compact, yet filled with charm. Another is a little larger, and incorporates the dining area into the kitchen. And here you see my own kitchen, today somewhat larger because I often have so many people visiting and so many guests to serve.

I believe that it's from our homes—and from our kitchens—that all of us go to meet the outside world. I recently saw a newspaper article whose headline read: "Home Is Where Leaders Are Made, Expert Says." A professor of human development at a major university had been interviewed about what he called his "passion for families" and his feelings that *families* hold the key to developing productive, happy, well-adjusted leaders.

This professor was speaking at a seminar as a consultant for corporations interested in how their employees could find personal satisfaction and excel. And this expert's conclusion, after years and years of study and research, was that the family was at the heart of all personal commit-

ment and excellence. What makes leaders? he was asked. What makes quality performers? Who teaches you what a good job is, what a shoddy job is? What makes people become happy, productive members of society? Again and again, the answer was *family.* That family environment of caring and concern, of support and understanding, provided a basis for later maturity and a foundation from which people could be flexible and deal with the uncertainties of their jobs without sacrificing their own personal standards.

It's just another reminder of the importance of the atmosphere you create in your home—no matter what your "home" may encompass, and whatever people it may include. You may be married and have children of your own; you may be widowed and have grandchildren or nieces and nephews; you may be single and have godchildren or lots of friends and "extended family" to love. But whatever situation you're in, experts say that "family" is the most excellent and effective framework in which people can care for and support each other and send well-adjusted people out into the world. This age-old collection of caring people—a family—prepare each other for doing a good job, cooperating in society, reaching out to help others.

To me, women are the thermostats of that home environment. A thermometer merely registers the temperature, but the thermostat *sets* it. What an exciting challenge and responsibility, setting a tone and establishing a value system based on a recognition and awareness of God's

Spirit and presence! If we can do this, our homes will truly be a haven instead of a hazard.

Love does have a locale on earth, and it's called home. And its benefits extend not only out into the world, but into your own innermost self as well. As James M. Barrie said, "Those who bring sunshine into the lives of others cannot keep it from themselves." *You'll* begin to glow, too, as you bring love into the lives of others.

Oh, yes, I love the kitchen. And even though there are mundane duties to be performed there day in and day out—potatoes to be peeled, pots to be scrubbed, ovens to be cleaned—the kitchen can still ring with joy and satisfaction. Sometimes the most humble objects—a collection of pine cones or a bowl of sunny lemons or a little vase filled with dried flowers—will be just what's needed to make you and others smile and go on. Maybe that verse you've stenciled on a cabinet or the plaque with a sunny saying will give somebody inspiration when they need it the most.

Do you have space in your kitchen for an old-fashioned rocker? There's no better way for relieving stress than rocking back and forth. If there are children around, by all means cuddle them there while you soothe their hurts and hear their stories and create a bond between you that will last a lifetime.

That spontaneous touch, that whimsical toy, that candle picked up on vacation that can be lit at night to burn away the cares of the day, that bowl of nuts with a beckoning nutcracker inviting somebody to crack the shells and pick out the moist meat. All these touches can make a big difference in a busy day.

Not every kitchen will be spacious, not everyone can have big baker's racks dangling with copper pans. Whether your space is large or small, whether you're having a Sunday morning breakfast for two or a late evening snack for several, your kitchen can be a place of refuge, of harmony, of beauty and charm.

It's out of the home—and out of the kitchen—that all of us go out to meet the world. But every kitchen should also say, "Come on in. Sit a spell. Let's share a magic moment in a busy day."

There are so many busy days, and so many magic moments. Let's make the most of them.

Our Exciting Heritage

4

I love learning about new things! As far as I'm concerned, picking up new knowledge and ideas and information is an endless, exciting adventure. I'm always sorry when I hear that people are frightened by terms like "French Provincial" or "Louis XIV" or "Chippendale." Please don't be intimidated, there's nothing to fear! These are all styles that are actually *fun* to know about, and can easily become a part of your own mood or decor.

Here and now I'd like to take you on a "tour" of the most well-known furniture styles and let you in on some fascinating tidbits about how famous people influenced those styles. Since this is a decorating book, a magic carpet seems the best way to travel. So have a seat while we go

overseas and back in time—all the way to Marco Polo.

In the thirteenth century, life in Europe was pretty bleak. Heavy, dark tapestries covered the walls, furniture was roughly hewn out of hunks of wood, even royalty ate from plates of wood or hammered pewter. Then the Italian adventurer Marco Polo sailed off and returned from the Orient with wondrous new goods— fabrics of bright colors, chests and

This dining room is resplendent with Chippendale reproductions.

chairs and other items that were lacquered and gilded, and colored plates made of porcelain. Plates so amazing and so desirable that all Europe wanted to copy them—and in country after country factories were set up to make . . . "china." That's how Wedgwood and Dresden and Delft began, each manufacturer developing his own special blue (the very blues that exist today) in an attempt to duplicate the Oriental hues carried back by Marco Polo.

For years the furnishings had been what we today call **Gothic**—massive, dark pieces with wrought iron hinges and leather straps, incredible chunks made for a hard life but certainly not for comfort or a pleasing appearance. But then from that point on, over the centuries, there was a gradual awakening all over Europe, an increased interest in music and art and learning—in the more uplifting and beautiful things in life.

And as this cultural Renaissance spread throughout the continent, people wanted furnishings that were more graceful and refined. As decades passed, these refinements became more and more elaborate, finally leading to an excessive style that came to be called **Baroque**—an outpouring of lavish carvings and ornate moldings that were used in palaces throughout Europe. And Louis XIV, whose name graces many of the elegant and romantically carved pieces of furniture we see today, filled his palace at Versailles with these gilded and fussy Baroque furnishings.

Then, toward the latter part of the eighteenth century, Louis XVI came to the throne. His wife was Marie Antoinette, and her tastes were more classically simple: She built a smaller residence for herself on the grounds

The graceful lines of the Queen Anne style are apparent in the lowboy and companion pieces in this setting.

The hand-crocheted tester and woven
bed covering are beautiful accompani-
ments to the functional antique pieces
in this room. The pewter ceiling fixture
and sconces add to the Early American
theme.

Twig furniture and accessories have a
special place in the American scene.
This four-poster bed displays the craft
of the artisan and combines well with
other rustic pieces to complete the
mood.

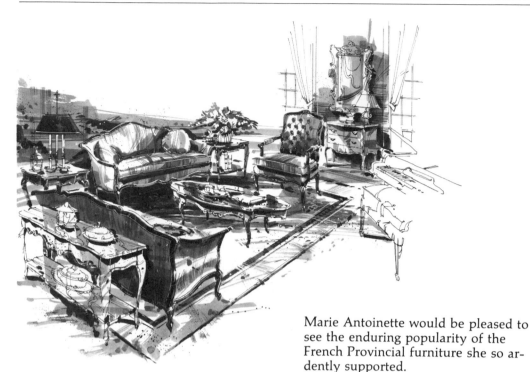

Marie Antoinette would be pleased to see the enduring popularity of the French Provincial furniture she so ardently supported.

of Versailles, a home called the Petite Trianon. And instead of filling it with ornate curlicues and Baroque details, she commissioned local workmen to make furnishings using woods such as walnut, beech, fruitwood, and pine, which were native to the area, in styles that were graceful and clean and simple. This was the "furniture of the provinces," and it gave the craftsmen of France a chance to develop and display their artistry. Nearly two centuries later, this style remains a very popular one—**French Provincial.**

Marie Antoinette started another wonderful trend, too. Not only did she ask the local people to make furniture, she asked them to make cotton fabrics to be used for draperies, wall hangings, and upholstery. They used the skins of the plentiful local grapes to make vivid dyes that colored cloth beautifully and set an example of using fresh and colorful patterns in the home.

After the French Revolution came the days of Napoleon—and he too had some influence on our modern decor. On one of his military campaigns, he returned to France by way of Rome and was impressed by some of the old Roman furnishings he saw there. They gave him the idea for a chair that could be folded up and taken along as he traveled, as well as for a sturdy chest with handsome brass hardware that would transport well, too. These items were the forerunners of the campaign chair (or director's chair, as it's sometimes called) and campaign chest that are still such popular favorites today.

Napoleon and his wife Josephine

also popularized certain emblems and decorations that are dear to us— none more so than the likeness of the eagle that is often seen embossed or carved on certain moldings or fixtures. An emblem using crossed swords (later adapted into "crossed palms") was another favorite of the emperor.

Let's move on to England. In the Middle Ages sturdy, nail-studded furniture was predominant. But William and Mary reigned as the seventeenth century slipped into the eighteenth and turned their castle into a real home by softening lines of furniture and giving rooms a more intimate and even homey look. Then

This bedroom ensemble worked in cherry and accented with brass hardware has long been a favorite in American homes.

came the **Queen Anne** period, during which chairs were padded and upholstered and became simply more *comfortable* than they had been for years.

In the last part of the eighteenth century, *Thomas Chippendale* became England's foremost furniture maker. Chippendale made his own sturdy modifications to the graceful Queen Anne style, creating sofas and chairs and chests, often in the mahogany he loved; he also introduced the English to many Chinese touches in his work. *Thomas Sheraton* and *George Hepplewhite* also developed classic designs that are beloved today in the twentieth century.

As far as the colonists of our own country were concerned, in the beginning their major concerns were food and shelter. The furnishings of

Stucco walls, tiled floor, embossed leather, and wrought iron identify this look as Mediterranean. The mirror, with its decorated tin frame, adds interest to the room.

the colonists' homes were at first very crude and made of cherry, pine, maple, and other woods of the New World that were close at hand. This **Early American** furniture continues to have lots of appeal in our modern day, made as it is with simple lines and good native wood.

But as America became established as a nation, some people began to import furnishings from France and other parts of Europe. And America developed its own skilled craftsmen. *Duncan Phyfe* was one of America's first great furniture makers (one of his trademarks was the beautiful lyre-back chair that we all recognize) and soon he and his compatriots were making furniture as fine as any in Europe.

The early American families didn't have carpet mills, so they took bits of wool and old clothing and braided them into rugs. They used candlelight, of course, and devised the idea of hanging the candle in a holder on the wall—and thus the sconce was created. It's interesting how challenges (some people call them problems, but I refuse) give us real opportunities and incentive to create wonderful new things.

Trends and styles have influenced us from other parts of the world as well. Especially in the West and Southwest of the United States, many people favor **Mediterranean** furniture, a term usually applied to Spanish or Mexican designs that may include carved or hand-tooled surfaces, nail-studding, geometric inlays, or wrought iron hardware or fixtures. It's a heavier, sturdier kind of furniture, but it's friendly, too; and many people in the West and Southwest enjoy it in their homes.

Modern furniture? Well, we all know what that is—generally chrome and stainless steel, items that gleam and glint—but you might hesitate to cozy up to them. Nonetheless, they can add a dramatic, high-tech touch to any setting; modern pieces of plastic, Plexiglas, Lucite, and vinyl are striking and durable without being bulky, and many people do favor them.

People sometimes confuse the term "modern" with "contemporary." **Contemporary,** however, covers a lot of territory: Contemporary refers to "the way things are done now"—and that often means a mixing of styles and periods in a relaxed way that's very "today." Contemporary furniture is sometimes sleek, sometimes sink-in-to-me-quick—but it's always functional, comfortable, clean of line, and without geegaws or clutter. Its straightforward character and honest strength make it a favorite for many families. And, once again, contemporary can include a wide assortment of other furniture families.

Those are some of the main classifications that you're likely to hear about as you assemble pieces to your own liking. If you want to know more (and I hope you do), take classes. Or browse through catalogues, magazines, antique shows, flea markets, and displays in furniture departments or stores. Visits to museums are wonderful opportunities to soak up information—many have actual room settings showing period arrangements. There's lots to know, and whole new worlds will open up to you. But above all, remember this: You don't *have* to be knowledgeable about every historic detail, you only need to know what pleases you ... and any additional information you pick up is fascinating icing on your decorating cake.

Now to the best news of all. You're not at all limited to any *one* of these styles. We live in the day of the *eclectic* look. That means anything goes, and does it ever! Even the grandest homes today have a blending of moods and periods. There are several combinations that seem especially popular today. The Mediterranean (or Spanish-Mexican) look is often seen combined with Early American or Contemporary furnishings: It's a marvelous juxtaposition of a heavier, handsome look with a more clean or airy one.

Another good grouping is when Oriental or Far Eastern styles are combined with Contemporary pieces or French Provincial pieces. And yet another grouping is some of the stately and fragile English classics with our heartier Early American pieces—and even some earthy Mediterranean pieces. By the way, if you have or are planning to have young children in your home, it's a marvelous idea to start out a young family on Early American pieces. They wear well and don't show scuffs and scratches. Then when children get older, you can add other styles that are somewhat more delicate and don't need protection from roughhousing or wear and tear.

One guideline though: When mix-

ing things in this way, it's generally best to let one style of furniture dominate, with pieces of other styles thrown in for contrast. If your room has truly equal amounts of two or three styles of furniture, the styles will fight each other for control, and a sense of harmony and charm will be lost.

With that in mind, let your heart —and imagination—take over. Whether you're rearranging or reassessing the furniture you've got, whether you're considering adding a brand-new piece to spice things up, whether you're in the enviable position of buying new things from scratch—pick what's appealing and practical for you. Don't be limited! (Even Marie Antoinette wasn't— along with all that attractive French Provincial furniture, she retained some gilded Baroque touches in the Petite Trianon.) If a single period piece appeals to you, and it's in proportion to and balanced with the rest of your room (more about this in the next chapter), add it. Classic French pieces, for example, are wonderful "accent pieces" because of the glamorous glint of gold they bring to a setting. A modern glass coffee table adds an accent of freedom and flair. A chunky Mediterranean chest can bring an airy room down to earth in an attractive way.

So if you've got a little bit of everything in your home, don't hang your head. You're as "in"—and interesting—as you could possibly be. And now on to some exciting ways to make what you've got work together and make your home a very special place indeed.

The Oriental theme is gaining in popularity, and its clean lines are evident in this breakfront and table grouping.

These modern modular units are grouped comfortably around an old campaign chest that doubles as a coffee table and storage piece.

Some Splendid Tips
for Getting Started

5

Now it's time to harvest your own pot of gold at the end of the color rainbow! But how—and where—to begin in your own home?

Look at what you like. Does the home of a friend—or a restaurant or hotel room—seem especially appealing? Well, really take note of what's been done to make the surroundings attractive. Go through books making note of what looks good to you, and why. Clip photos from magazines, start a looseleaf notebook to hold pictures and gather notations about decorating ideas that seem to work, that appeal to you. Some big department stores have show areas in which they display carefully assembled rooms. Take a look and figure out what's been done. Could you do it too in your own home?

Become a collector of swatches and paint color cards and fabric samples and wallpaper pieces that please you. Arrange and rearrange them to see how they go together. Spread them out and show to family or friends to get their reactions about what appeals. Staple all these swatches in your notebook so you can go back to them whenever you need to plan or think—or just dream.

Get everybody in on the act. Talk things over with others in the house. If you're mad about mocha but it makes your husband feel blah, then come up with another color; you want elements that everyone can live with . . . and *like*. I always say that people were made to be loved and things were made to be used. We get into trouble when we reverse this and begin to love things and use people. So no matter how involved you get in your decorating, remember that the interests and happiness of family and friends far surpass any satisfactions you get from any material objects or decorations.

Trust yourself. Don't be swayed by what's in fashion or what experts or others tell you you should like. Just because bitter orange or sweet-pea purple is all the rage *this* year doesn't mean "fashion leaders" will be able to stand the sight of it the next—or, more to the point, that *you'll* want it around for that long. So check others for advice, opinions, and ideas, but when it's time to decide, the choice is yours. Follow your instinct—it's excellent.

It used to bother me when people would take something *I* didn't like and insist it belonged in their home. I used to think, "I'd better reeducate them." But then I of course realized that what each person wants is what he or she needs around them. If a piece says to them, "Take me home," then that's the way it should be. This is the quarrel I have with many professional decorators: They want to put *their* mark on a home without regard for what a family needs and wants to make them feel good.

One more thing about trusting yourself: Don't panic if you *can't* seem to come to a decision about what colors or patterns or styles you want. Peter Marshall delivered a prayer once that went like this: "Teach us how to listen to the prompting of Thy Spirit, and thus save us from floundering in indecision that wastes time, subtracts from our peace, divides our efficiency and multiplies our troubles." Well, I think that applies to everyday decisions as well as big ones, to "little" choices, too. If you're in a dither about what to do, be still and say a small prayer. After all, you *want* God's Spirit in your home and surroundings—so if you need help, ask for it.

Try a new perspective. Go out of your house and come in through your front door as though you've never been there before. What do you see? Signs of people who are interesting and alive—or maybe a little bit stodgy and dull? Look at your surroundings with fresh eyes—and evaluate.

Ask friends whose taste appeals to

you for advice and appraisal. Tell them you'd like a frank—but of course kindly—evaluation of how you might improve your decor. Here's another way to get a different view of the rooms you see every day: Look in a mirror! Take a nice big one and look over your shoulder at all those familiar places you live in. Somehow the mirror image allows you to see the whole picture that you're just too close to otherwise.

Pause to be practical. As you mull over the rooms you want to revamp or spruce up, think your way through a typical day. Will kids and pets be dashing through? Then polished floors and satiny cushions aren't the answer. Is it a room where people study, read, relax? Then this isn't the place for mustard-colored walls and jingling wind chimes. Project your thoughts into the future and think about how any changes you're considering will really look and feel in the months and years ahead.

Take your color "temperature." When people come to me unsure of what colors suit them or which ones they can actually live with, I suggest they go to the dime store and get inexpensive squares of chiffon in a variety of colors. Drape these squares around you, leave them strewn around on sofas, chair backs, even stick them to the wall with masking tape. See how they make you *feel*. To me, *the true test of whether a color's right for you is if it makes you light up from within.* How a color makes you feel is much more important than how it impresses neighbors or how you *wished* it made you feel.

A floor plan is fun. If you're planning a major overhaul for a room, or if you're actually starting from scratch in a new home or country place, get some graph paper and mark out the dimensions of your room. Figure that every block on the paper represents a square foot, and mark off the correct places for all windows, doors, fireplaces. Make cardboard cutouts of furniture, rugs, plants that you're considering rearranging, or moving from other parts of the house, or buying. Move figures around to see if they really will fit in the setting in which you envision them, and map out the "traffic flow" in these areas. Is there enough room for children, visitors, even party guests (if you're a party giver) to move around comfortably? Be sure you've left enough room for closet doors to open, for access to bureaus and storage areas.

Once again, get all family members excited and involved. Let them know how much you want *them* to be happy in their surroundings. Your enthusiasm will be contagious and help make everyone more sensitive to the beautiful elements that are all around us and can be brought into our own rooms and homes.

Keep your balance. Even if you're making changes in only one room of the house, remember that what you do has got to integrate with the whole living area. Especially if it's a living room or dining room or other area that "flows" into other spaces, be sure that any colors or styles or moods you create in one place won't clash or be out of harmony with

Charming is the word for this young girl's room (*above*). Fabric is the inexpensive and unifying element—on the window, wall, and bed.

Assembling fabric swatches, wall-covering samples, and paint colors should be an early step in any decorating plan. All materials should be viewed in the lighting in which they will be used.

others. This sense of balance, by the way, should be applied to any individual room itself: Don't "tear things apart" by doing a bit of something here, then jumping to another unrelated scheme or color there. Whatever you do, always keep balancing so that no one element is so overwhelming that it throws the whole room out of whack.

There's one sure way of uniting everything in your home, and it's one of my very favorite techniques that I recommend to everyone. Use the same wall-to-wall carpeting—same color, same texture—throughout your entire house. Then no matter what your decor in individual rooms, the carpeting will bring everything together in one comfortable sweep. This is a wonderful trick to use if your home seems broken up into a living area here, a kitchen area there, a dining area off in a corner. Or in the upstairs an expanse of the same color carpet will draw all rooms together and give your home a cohesive, finished look—no matter what seemingly discordant elements are in individual rooms or areas.

Let cherished things inspire you. If you really don't know where to start or if too many fabulous color choices have your head whirling, pick up on the colors in a favorite picture or poster, or in those patterned curtains that you especially love. Or use the hues in a multicolored rug or a beloved quilt as a starting point, and let them be the basis for your color scheme.

Patterned fabrics too are often a starting point—perhaps you've seen

a floral or geometric design that you long to use in drapes or pillows. Allow these colors to inspire you. Is there a wash of peach in the pattern? Perhaps a peach tint would be luscious on your walls. Is the pattern flecked with dots of honey gold? That color could be right for sink-in-and-sigh slipcovers. Does the fabric pattern have rosy stripes? A rosy accent in pillows or a vase or figurines could be in order.

By following the color schemes that experts have already put together (and that *you* like, too) in fabrics, wallpapers, dishes, even in a favorite scarf or dress, you'll have sure-fire color success.

In other words, follow your heart and pick something you like—and let *it* set off your creative impulses. This is definitely a place to play favorites. *Your* favorites.

If the big picture overwhelms you, look at a smaller one. Too often people decide that there's so much to do that they shouldn't do anything at all. Not true! Even the littlest touch can transform your home—and your spirits. Maybe you can't change your sofa or chairs or knock down the walls and start completely over. But remember that a coat of paint works wonders in giving entire rooms (or individual pieces of furniture) a sparkling new look. Also remember those great tricks with white we told you about in chapter two.

And if you're not up to a paint job at the moment, you can give the looks of any room a lift by using accessories. (Great ideas for those are coming up in a few pages.)

A family heirloom such as this cup-
board can serve a decorative as well as
a utilitarian purpose.

Raiding the attic can sometimes yield
hidden treasures. Unusual pieces lend
visual interest while aiding the budget.

Wall-to-wall carpeting unifies this split-level condominium, while the white background and furnishings "expand" the area.

Take risks. If something calls out to you and says, "Take me home," and it's not completely out of the question as far as your budget and other surroundings are concerned, grab the object and make it your own. Don't be afraid that people will laugh at you and say, "She's crazy." I've never let that stop me from doing things other people thought wouldn't work. In fact, when I started my company *Home Interiors and Gifts,* a lot of people thought we wouldn't be able to make that work either. So I've never been stopped by a fear that I'd fall flat on my face or that people would laugh at me. I was born on April Fools' Day, and I'm ever grateful that the Lord took care of that for me right away. I've never been held back by the fear that I'd do something other people thought was foolish. I just go ahead and try everything!

Remember B.U.S. No, that's not a system of transportation. It's Balance, Unity, and Scale—three elements that any home decorator has to keep in mind.

Balance means keeping furnishings and colors spread evenly throughout a room so no one area looks lopsided. You wouldn't, for instance, mass all your huge, heavy pieces at one end of the dining room, or jam every one of your pictures on a single wall. Keep color and furniture and objects arrayed in such a way that the entire scene is in proportion and evenly distributed.

Unity means that each object seems to belong, to fit in with other elements in the room to create an over-

all feeling of harmony. This doesn't mean you can't spontaneously add elements or accents that are delightfully different. But it means your "big picture" does have to be unified: Sleek contemporary furniture just doesn't go with country-flowered wallpaper and wrought iron Spanish grillwork. Follow the basic combinations of color and furnishings I've told you about, and you won't have any visitors going, "Ouch!" and covering their eyes when they come to call.

Scale means the relationship that all items in your room have to one another and to the room itself. It's not right to cram massive, overstuffed furniture into a small study; a vast loftlike space will simply swallow up less substantial furniture or delicate antiques. And in any size room, if frail-looking items are placed alongside more gargantuan pieces, the overall look will simply not be right.

Look to the light. Make sure you evaluate the swatches and samples and colors you select in the actual light of the room or area they'll appear in. Colors may be brighter or paler or simply *not* what you expect, when they're actually in your home. So check things out ... in natural daylight, in evening hours, under overhead lights or fluorescents.

Don't think you have to rush. Doing things step by step, bit by bit, is not only fine—but it actually may be *more* satisfying to develop your decor slowly. That way you can let each new change "settle" while you decide what you want next—and you'll have the time and energy to savor each new addition. Gradual changes are also easier on the budget. So don't push yourself. Everything will evolve and fall into place as it's supposed to—*when* it's supposed to. Remember, God leads not by miles but by inches.

Start now. Two little words that make the big difference. Even if it's just in the smallest way, the tiniest detail, don't keep waiting until "tomorrow" to "do something" to your home. Begin now and the momentum will build ... to wonderful results!

"I Have This Wall . . ."

Over the years my staff and I have met with countless people in order to help solve their decorating dilemmas. And again and again we'll hear the same perplexed statement: "I have this wall . . . and just don't know what to do with it."

I guess we shouldn't be surprised. In any room, there are more *walls* than anything else. And what's *on* them is incredibly important to the entire look—and mood—of your house or apartment. I once heard an expert estimate that most people remember 11 percent of what they hear, but over 70 percent of what they *see*. So your pictures and plaques, your wallcoverings and window treatments all give visitors a message. And make a lasting impression on the people who live within those four walls—as well as on you yourself.

Since decorating is entertaining the eye, it follows that walls should be "entertaining" too. And all the walls of a room should work together to give an entire look of harmony and completeness. So to begin with, let me give you an overview of what you'll be trying to accomplish as you make your own walls look wonderful.

Preparing the Surface

Before talking about all the pretty things that go *on* your walls, let's talk about the surface of the walls themselves. Walls wrap their arms around your room and create a mood that can be serene—or scintillating. The atmosphere they establish is important. What can you do to make them brighter, or bolder, or cozier, or smarter? Today it's possible to buy such an incredible variety of colors and coverings that you can have walls that aren't like anyone else's and that express your own individuality and creativity.

Get along, old paint. Never forget that paint is one of the easiest and most economical ways to bring new life to a room. Maybe you want to paint all four walls a happy new color, maybe you want to paint one wall (or even a part of a wall) in a cheery accent color. Or perhaps you want to paint walls one color—and ceilings, wainscoting, mantels, and sills of doors and windows another color altogether. What a lot you can do!

Do you want your walls to keep a low profile? Then paint them in soft, easygoing colors that seem to recede rather than leap out at you. When walls are bathed in subtle tones, they're less noticeable and create an atmosphere that's more low-key and relaxed.

If you want walls to stand out and be real focal points of drama and interest, use bolder, brighter colors to bring them front and center. As I've said before, for me a little of the "Yippee!" colors goes a long way. But a touch here and there does add zest to a room, and certain more muted shades of red and orange *can* add a note of needed cheer.

If you want the emphasis to be on your furniture and not on your walls, then whites and creams and neutrals are the colors to pick. Or paint walls in a tint that's just a whisper of one of the colors in your overall decor.

Many people opt for painting their own walls, and you should be able to pick up both the materials and the advice you need at your local paint or hardware store. Basically, there are two types of indoor paint today: latex (water-base) or alkyd (oil-base). Latex is favored for its easy cleanup and quick-drying qualities. Alkyd, on the other hand, especially alkyd enamel, will provide a harder finish for woodwork and walls that get tougher treatment—in kitchen and bathroom, for instance. There are "textured paints" that have additives that rough them up—and can be applied to give a wall a rough or stucco surface.

Paint has different finishes, too. *High-gloss* gives a lacquered or enameled look that's dramatic—and easy to clean. *Semi-gloss* means a surface that's satiny but not overpowering; fingerprints, smudges, and ordinary wear and tear will wipe off without a lot of scrub and fuss. And a *flat* finish is more muted, comfortable looking without a lot of sheen (but will take more scrub-a-dubbing to keep clean).

If you're doing it yourself (and today most people do, especially now that we have rollers), get advice from your paint store. Then tie up your hair, cover up the furniture and floor (*all* of it—no matter how neat you think you're going to be, you'll still splatter), and whistle while you work (that's not meant to be whimsical advice, it's very practical).

What about wallpaper? Wallpaper can give a special wake-up touch to any room, and there's an impressive and incredible selection of patterns and styles and colors available in stores today. When picking wallpaper for a room, the same basic color principles apply: Darker colors and smaller prints will close in a room, making it appear smaller and cozier; lighter colors and larger patterns will open up a room, making it seem more spacious and airy.

Many wallpapers nowadays are *prepasted*, which means you cut panels to fit, then wet the back, and maneuver paper onto walls. Otherwise it's up to you (or professional paperhangers) to apply the paste, and this can be more of a job than many home decorators are up to. So unless you have lots of patience, I'd suggest checking labels immediately for that "prepasted" marking.

In addition to "paper" wallpapers, there are also *washable wall coverings*—and this means coverings of vinyl or plastic or other synthetics that wipe clean quickly with a sponge (some are even marked "scrubbable" for real trouble areas). There are also wall coverings of fabric, burlap, felt, cork, grass cloth, and gleaming Mylar; and these can add extra texture or dimension to a room.

To add to the fun, many wallpapers and wall coverings today come coordinated with fabrics for curtains, window shades, even slipcovers—so check into this too.

Here's a wonderful way to "frame" a room. Use *border trims* of wallpaper that are available in many stores. These colorful strips may be covered with stripes or dots or tiny flowers or berries, or with barnyard animals or cartoon characters just right for a nursery. Border trims are anywhere from several inches to a foot wide, and you can slip them onto your walls just below ceiling level, around wainscoting, along windows or sills. Many of these come with matching papers or fabrics for curtains or cushions and provide even more delightful possibilities for a room.

Surprise yourself with stencils. This is a lovely old-fashioned touch that many decorators have rediscovered. A variety of stencils are now available in paper and plastic at many art-supply and craft stores, or you can cut designs yourself out of sturdy paper. You can stencil flowers, or charming cross-hatching, or even art deco designs on walls—even floors and furniture. Frame windows

Bonjour!/Bonjour! Border/Gigi copyright © Katzenbach & Warren, Inc.

and doors with stenciling; run it as a border along ceilings or floors. Fasten stencils down with masking tape so they won't slip, fill in carefully with latex or acrylic paints, then remove the stencil carefully and allow to dry.

Other clever cover-ups. Yards of *fabric* can be stretched or shirred over one or all of your walls to wrap your room in a cocoon of color. Spread out the fabric and fasten to walls with Velcro or double-edged tape. Or attach curtain rods at ceiling and floor, and shirr fabric in between. You can drape off an alcove in a bedroom or around a window seat. Hang curtains on a rod from the ceiling, then sweep them back and fasten. Just imagine, cushions, curtains, wallpaper, all coordinated in a charming country pattern in a study or sitting room!

Bamboo can be bought in rolls and hung at the top of a wall—then unfurled to the floor and attached at the bottom (tack it at various places throughout to keep it secure against the wall). *Mats* or *rugs* can cover entire walls, too—so can *carpeting.* There are also sheets of *paneling* in laminated veneers of wood or brick; other possibilities are plywood or pegboard.

And don't forget *quilts.* Cut a length of wood to a quilt's width, fasten it next to the ceiling, tack the quilt to that. Or attach cafe-curtain rings to the quilt's top edge, and string it along a curtain rod that you've attached to the top of the wall.

Adding a Smile to Your Walls

During the Depression I found myself alone, a single parent, struggling to raise two young children. I think the reason that time was called the Depression was that life was so depressing. The way we decorated our homes then was by choosing one of the illustrated calendars distributed by the feed stores and lumberyards. We never even thought of buying a painting or mirror or anything else to hang on the wall that would make our hearts sing. It was simply out of the question.

Today, though, we have so many blessings. We *are* able to buy things that bring us pleasure, to fill the four walls that surround us with treasures that lift our spirits and remind us that God's beauty is everywhere, especially in our homes And although there are fine things underfoot and overhead, it's walls that face us again and again as we go about our days. Let's take a look now at what we can put on them.

Pretty as a picture. A picture is worth a thousand words. And a thousand good feelings too. Hang pictures alone. Or in combination with others. As one good-sized and dramatic focal point. Or as a collection of smaller pictures, perhaps in an arrangement of other items that make a complete and charming array. The pictures you choose can be

Imaginative use of the coordinating border trim accents the dramatic black and white color scheme of this bedroom.

prints or oils or etchings, they can be folk art or family-sketched treasures or reproductions of art you enjoy. But whatever you pick, pictures are an important part of any wall.

Pictures can go anywhere. Turn a long, narrow hallway into a gallery by displaying a collection of art or photos. Decorate bathroom walls with framed turn-of-the-century women's magazine covers, fill kitchens with watercolors of fruit and vegetables, fill the wall by a staircase with delightful framed posters or colorful cards you've picked up on vacation. Whatever your taste or mood or location, you'll find pictures to fill the space.

Find a frame that fits. A frame can be as important as the picture itself. So make sure your frames don't clash with your subject matter (or the rest of your room for that matter) or overpower your picture. Larger pictures or heavier-looking oil paintings can take weightier and more complicated frames; etchings or sketches or watercolors with a lighter, more fragile air require simpler frames that go along with their spirit.

Remember that you don't want your pictures to sink right into the wall, or be swallowed up or be unnoticeable. So choose a frame that contrasts with the wall it will be on. Make sure your frame stands out against the wallpaper or paneling or paint. Some specific tips: If your wallpaper is in a "busy" pattern, keep your frames and the subject matter of your pictures simpler. If you're hanging pictures on wood paneling, remember that paneling really soaks up color, and a frame

and picture have to be especially bold to stand out; a metal frame (silver or copper or gold) will be especially effective in this situation.

Mats are a marvelous way to glamorize otherwise unassuming pictures. Even a quiet little scene or drawing, when set off by a colorful mat, can look alive and important. Keep in mind that the color of the mat (or the background on which you're placing your picture or antique postcard or pressed flowers) can be "pulled" from other items or accessories in the room.

There's one fabulous source of art that I want to be sure to mention. It's your own favorite first-graders—or budding high-school artists. Art done by even the youngest children— whether they're your own children or grandchildren or nieces or nephews, or young neighbors who drop by to visit—can add a bright and beguiling touch to any surroundings. And when artwork like this is properly framed and displayed, the spirit of the young artist will receive an important and unforgettable boost.

I'd like to add, by the way, that framing your own treasures can be a wonderful fun activity for family and friends. Today you can buy frames of all shapes and sizes. Or rummage around in the attic or basement and see what wondrous old frames you can find to clean up or strip and refinish. Then add mats and backgrounds of lively colors or delightful scraps of fabric that coordinate with your room's decor. Everybody will have fun participating in this activity and can enjoy such efforts for years afterward—and that's what Decorating With Love is all about, isn't it?

If you're not particularly interested in matting and framing your own art, or if you're unsure about choosing the right frame, you'll be glad to know that nowadays there's an incredible and appealing range of pictures and reproductions that come already framed and ready to go on your wall. Do you want a nature scene, tranquil and serene? Delightful pictures of individuals, of all ages, portrayed in thoughtful or joyous moments? A soothing still life or captivating animal scene or floral arrangement—or inspirational scene of religious beauty? All these and many more *are* available, already placed in the proper frame by experts. So be on the lookout for these too as you pick and choose pictures for your home.

In family rooms, bedrooms, dens, recreation rooms, even bathrooms—in any special place that is dear to you—you can, of course, use photographs of your immediate or extended family. Or what about that long hallway or stairway we mentioned before? Here's an excellent place to create a gallery and hang photo after beloved photo. Have these, too, framed attractively. Often you can show family and friends and pets as they are growing up and changing, and at various exciting events in their lives.

Nowadays we live in *all* our homes. There's no one particular room that's set aside for getting together the way the parlor used to be. So enjoy yourself. Put pictures of your family and friends wherever you (and they) enjoy them. Those "official" portraits, too—weddings, formal family "sittings," graduations—can also be placed wherever everyone will enjoy them most, as long as the entire portrait and frame go with the scale and balance and composition in the rest of the room.

Mirror, mirror—make some magic! I love to use mirrors. They make everything so exciting, give things that extra twinkle—and trick people (in the nicest way possible) into "seeing" more than they actually are. Here's how:

Mirrors can make you see double. Place mirrors in such a way that they cast back the reflection of attractive areas or objects. This will give you twice the viewing pleasure. Now of course you don't want to place a mirror so that it reflects back a room's architectural defect, or a corner or crevice that isn't particularly interesting. But, oh, if that mirror is reflecting back an entire area of an attractive room, or on a smaller scale is reflecting back a stunning figurine or plant or painting—well then you've got double vision of the loveliest sort.

Open things up—it's done with mirrors! Large mirrors may be used to fool the eye by making smaller rooms look larger. This is a trick that works well in tiny foyers, cramped dining alcoves, and narrow hallways. You can get mirrors that will cover an entire wall. Or large "sheets" of mirror that can go over a mantel or over just the upper half of a wall. Here is a good device to use in a dining room or area: Put the table against the wall;

How effective this hand-painted panel above the fireplace is in imparting a unique charm to this romantic bedroom (*above left*).

Growing in popularity is the perpendicular use of wall-covering borders that traditionally are run only horizontally (*below left*). Here they coordinate with the fabric on the bed and table.

The use of mirrored panels in this comfortably formal room make it dance with sunlight during the day and glow with romance at night (*above*).

then a mirror next to and above it will make the table look twice as large.

Smaller mirrors, too, of different sizes and shapes can be clustered together to reflect back certain areas. Over the years I've often suggested to people that they use five or seven or nine smaller mirrors "bumper to bumper" across a wall over a sofa or over a mantel. It creates a dramatic and thrilling effect.

Mirrors turn on the light. In the days before electricity, mirrors served a very practical purpose—they reflected back the light from candles, and some enterprising person put mirror and candle together on the wall in something called a sconce.

Today when mirrors are placed so that they bounce back either natural light, electric light, or candlelight, the mood of the room is really affected. Because of mirrors, rooms dance with sunlight during the day; they glow with romance and coziness at night. An added bonus: You'll actually save on your light bill if people don't have to flick on a switch every time they pass through a dim hallway or room.

Mirrors have many faces. Not only do they stand (or hang) alone, but mirrors also come as part of wall hangings, shelves, drawers, sconces, and other accessories. And then the figurines or plants or candles or floral arrangements or groupings are given double the visual excitement.

What kinds of mirrors are there? First of all, mirrors can be either concave (in which the mirror curves slightly inward, and therefore tends to magnify the objects it reflects) or convex (the mirror face curves outward, so that the area that is reflected is increased). Many antique mirrors are convex, and today so are many mirrors used for security purposes.

Mirrors sometimes will be beveled—they'll have a polished edge of about half an inch cut at a slant to the main mirror area. Beveled mirrors can only reflect what's directly across from them and are often without a frame.

Framed mirrors are available in many designs and sizes and shapes. Frames may be made of metal or wood. Today there are many frames made of composite materials or molded plastics that still have the look and heft of wood or metal, but are actually lighter in weight and easier to handle.

In addition to real antiques, there are also mirrors today that have been treated to have an antique look. The glass in these mirrors has been treated to create a smoky or shadowy effect, and the frames too have been "stressed" to appear veiny and mottled.

An antique look always adds special richness to a home. And if you find a *real* antique mirror, all the better. The glass in the mirror itself may not be of great quality—but the old frame and the entire impression the mirror makes may be irresistible. So if you come upon an antique mirror that strikes your fancy in your attic or a flea market, it's nice to use it.

Shelve it! If you want a wall to reach out and make people take notice, add a shelf—or several. Shelves add a definite third dimension to a wall. They might stand alone as a single shelf that holds figurines or flower arrangements. Or they could be a series of shelves linked together. Combined with pictures, mirrors, or assorted hanging memorabilia, the arrangement can add depth, texture, and balance to an otherwise bland wall. Shelves can be teak or oak or mahogany; they can include glass or brass; and they can be backed by mirrors to reflect whatever wonders the shelves hold.

For real drama, hang three to five shelves of the same size and style. Line them up symmetrically, or work out on paper a balanced scheme for placing the shelves in a pleasing pattern. Such arrangements can be used instead of a bookcase or etagere to hold lovely belongings and flowers and candles and books.

Speaking of *books*, I love them and use them and have many in my home. Books in a home tell something exciting about the people who live there. However, I'm reminded of the story of the woman who went into a bookstore and asked for three yards of green books to go with the decorating scheme in her living room. Whether the story is true or not, I don't know—but it does illustrate the mistaken attitude some people have about books. Books are not simply decorative objects. They're priceless containers of knowledge and insight and beauty and humor and pleasure—I could go on and on. So display them with pride—but *read* them, too!

Other items for display. Any number of wondrous things can be clustered on your walls, either in groupings of their own or among the other items we've just mentioned. Plaques with favorite or inspirational sayings bring light to everyone's life. Sconces hold candles that cast a lovely light. Sculpted forms of birds, flowers, butterflies—many charming items are available.

Keep in mind that what you hang can be practical as well as pleasing. Some examples: kitchen utensils—polished and pretty pots and pans—hung on kitchen and pantry walls (gleaming copper ones can even go on dining room walls). Tools—either ones you use, or interesting antique ones. Musical instruments—why keep guitars or banjos or even trombones and tambourines tucked away

in cumbersome cases? Hang them as part of your wall display. And what about hats? Some people have fanciful collections of everything from fire fighters' hats and pith helmets to sombreros and plumed bonnets; but even if your hats are less exotic, if they're nice to look at, hang them up.

Other charming yet practical items to add to your wall display: stately or unusual clocks (including cuckoos), fantastic fans, interesting baskets (the kind without handles that go flat against the wall), woven wreaths, folk art wood carvings, fabulous old weather vanes. Jewelry can make an artistic display, too; tack it up on a wall, perhaps with beaded bags, belts, anything that's unusual and attractive.

Some people even drape and display the clothes they wear. You could run a curtain rod through the sleeves and across the shoulders of a kimono with beautiful embroidery, then display it over a bed or in a powder room. Whatever's in your closet or kitchen, your cellar or attic—bring it out, drape it against the wall, and try it out with other items, and if it pleases you, by all means hang it up.

Here's a real space saver. Do as the Shakers did and hang ladder-back chairs high on the wall. It keeps them out of the way when not in use and gives an old-fashioned kitchen or dining room a touch of old-time charm.

Let your imagination run free. Use items you like, that reflect your interests—whether specially purchased or drawn from your belongings—and your walls will surely smile. Let's talk now about the actual arrangement of these selections.

Happy Hang-ups,
Wonderful Walls

7

Now that we've looked at some of the many items that can be used to enhance our walls, let's consider how to present them in the best possible way.

How Wall Groupings Enhance Your Decorating Scheme

First of all, they add *color*—that incredible element that does so much to enrich your surroundings. Even if an accessory on the wall does no more than pick up on and add a bit more emphasis to a color in your room—well, that alone is an important factor in your overall design plan.

Second, wall hangings (or sculptures or sconces or figurines or shelves) add *texture* to a room. They can add the contrast that is so often needed to warm up a room and make it more interesting. If your room has wood-paneled walls or wood furniture, for instance, you need the contrast of polished silver, brass, or copper on the walls, as well as the glint of mirrors or the crispness of a lacquered plaque.

Then there's *dimension.* When you hang shelves or sconces on your walls, when you add relief sculptures or contoured items, your walls have an appealing nubbiness that interests the eye and makes things come alive.

The Focal Wall

Generally speaking, each room should have a "focal wall," the first wall you see when you enter a room—the wall that ties the entire room together. This wall may be one with a natural dominating element like a fireplace or bookcase—or one to which the eye is drawn by the artful arrangement of furniture and accessories.

Remember B.U.S.

If you want your wall arrangements to excite the senses, keep in mind the B.U.S. principles I mentioned before—balance, unity, and scale. These elements are so important that they bear repeating once again.

Balance by making sure your wall grouping isn't wildly thrown all over your wall, or "loaded" in such a lop-

sided way that the wall or arrangement seems to be "tilting" in one direction. Make sure the objects you array have a rhythm, a distribution in weight and size that unifies a wall rather than pulls it apart. This, by the way, doesn't mean all your wall hangings have to be centered or hung in a symmetrical way—not at all. It just means that all accessories on the entire wall must finally balance out into a pleasing whole. If you've hung a large picture or poster or painting over your sofa to the right, you must balance things out by placing a tall lamp or plant on an end table to the left. If you're planning a grouping of smaller items, cluster them in such a way that a larger sconce on the right, for instance, is clustered with perhaps two smaller plaques on the left.

Achieve *unity* by using only items that "go together"—and, believe me, your own eye and instincts will tell

you this sooner or later. By the way, it's fine if you realize this *later* rather than sooner. Sometimes you actually have to live with something and see it for a while to know whether it "goes" or not. Most of you, though, will realize that a heavy oil painting with a huge, ornate frame doesn't belong with a metal-framed modern print; or that your young son's *Star Wars* posters don't belong over the sideboard in the dining room alongside some pretty, old-fashioned sconces. Group your objects so that no one overwhelms the others and all have a common theme or look or element that binds them together (such as similar frames, or colored mats, or period style).

Keep everything in *scale* by making sure what's on the wall is big enough (or small enough) for the room. Little bitty plaques don't belong over an enormous overstuffed sofa, a wide expanse of mirror in a hulking frame doesn't belong in a smaller room over fragile-looking French Provincial furniture.

Let me tell you again, though (because I can't tell you enough), to please not be intimidated by any of this advice. Right now you may be thinking, "Maybe I don't *know* what's in scale, what belongs and what doesn't." All right, even if that's a little bit true (and it probably isn't), don't worry. Even if you do miss in any of these areas, there's plenty of time later to switch or rearrange or replace or try something different. Nothing is set in stone, even the most horrendous decorating mistake. (And even something that's considered "officially awful" can be fun to try for

a while.) So plunge right in and enjoy yourself!

Now here's another tip: Be sure in your wall arrangements to "bring things down to earth" at some point. The eye moves upward and across a wall but then needs to be brought to rest at some point near the floor. Don't leave the viewers' gaze hanging—leaving the illusion that they've been flung off into space. "Ground" your wall arrangement by placing an object such as a large plant somewhere alongside sofa or chair or table in your grouping. A floor lamp or paneled screen would serve the same purpose.

How close should various items on your wall be? It's a good rule of thumb to keep the parts of your grouping close enough together that the eye can move smoothly from one to another. Generally speaking,

Hogatta®, Duke's Stripe®, Andrews Stripe®, copyright Greeff Fabrics, Inc.

Pick a theme and make it yours. This
one is nautical and nice.

B.U.S. are preserved in this two-story
grouping of framed prints and objets
d'art.

nothing should be placed farther apart in a grouping than half its diameter. Think of each grouping as having an invisible frame around it; this image should help you keep your items at the appropriate distance from one another.

Gather together the items you're considering and spread them on the floor or a table to see how they look together. And then try this marvelous little trick of the trade that we've used at *Home Interiors and Gifts* over the years.

Put It Down on Paper

Take a nice large piece of brown paper and arrange your pictures, plaques, or mirrors on that. Think of each grouping as a single unit, and move your items around until they achieve the right balance and compo-

sition you want. When you have a pleasing arrangement, mark on the paper the places where nails should be driven. Then place the paper against the wall, and drive your nails through those pencil marks. When you rip the paper away, you'll have the nails just where you decided you want them. This will save you a lot of trial and error *on* the wall itself—and will certainly save you a lot of nail holes in the wrong places.

As far as the actual hammering is concerned, if you have plaster walls put a bit of adhesive tape over the spot where you intend to drive the nail. When you hammer, this will keep the plaster from crumbling and the nail hole from disintegrating.

At What Height Should You Hang Accessories?

Well, first of all, let me ask you: Is your room a "standing room" or a "sitting room"—or a combination of both? A "standing room" is a room like an entrance way or hallway that you pass through—but aren't likely to actually sit down and stay in. And a "sitting room" then is obviously a room where you sit down to relax, or eat, or chat, or visit . . . such as the living room or den or dining area.

Often people fail to consider this when arranging their wall hangings. So keep things at a higher eye level in places where passersby will be "upright." And drop them to a lower eye level where lookers are more likely to be sitting. How to tell where that level is? Just sit down and look yourself—really look. When you're settled on the sofa, what—and where

—do you see? That's the place and the level to start hanging wall decorations.

Eye level is also important when you are trying to achieve a certain mood, whether it's soft and homey or more formal and elegant. If you're trying to create a cozy feeling, hang items lower. But if you want something not quite as personal, you might prefer to hang your accessories or pieces of art a bit higher.

But not *too* high. If your eye has to travel *too* far upward, the unity you want to exist between wall and furniture will be thrown off. If you've got to tilt your head back to see an object clearly, or if you have the feeling that something is overhead instead of at comfortable eye level—then lower it!

Here's something else to consider. Will people be sitting against the wall on which you've assembled your accessories? If you're hanging items over a sofa or some comfortable chairs, be sure all items are high enough that people don't knock their heads when leaning back. The same applies for articles hung over headboards. Just imagine getting into bed with the intention of leaning back and reading a new book—and ending up vying for space with a picture frame. You want everyone in the house to be comfortable—including yourself—so check and see just where people's heads are going to come while sitting down. And hang objects *above* that point.

"Pull" Colors to Use in Your Wall Groupings

That means choosing items for your walls that pick up on colors already in your decorating scheme—a rosy red in the pattern of your sofa's upholstery, a bird's egg blue in a porcelain figure on the coffee table, a jade green woven in a nubby throw rug, a blaze of yellow in a piece of Indian pottery. Pick up on these colors and repeat them in what you hang. And depending on which colors you "pull," you can warm or cool the mood of your room accordingly. If a warm look is what you want in winter, pull russets and reds and apricots and hang wall accessories that contain those colors. Then in summer, when you'd like a cooler look, pull greens and blues and switch to accessories that contain these cooler colors. Here again, with wall accessories, you can change them to suit the seasons . . . and give the look of your home a new lift.

Hand-painted tiles "pulled" from the
floral pattern of the fabric decorate the
fireplace and illustrate so well how ingenuity can enhance a room setting.

The colors in the oil painting set the
color scheme for this contemporary living room—subtle, soft, and serene.

NO

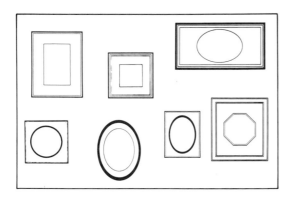

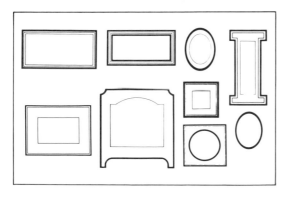

Arranging How-to

Now for some tips about *how* to arrange those groupings—whether you're using pictures or mirrors or sconces . . . or whatever pleases you.

Keep your items orderly. Some people tack pictures or other hangings on their walls willy-nilly; and although that may have a certain wild charm, more often than not it just looks a mess. That's why I think it's a good idea to hang your *entire* arrangement in the basic shape of a square or rectangle. The outer items in your arrangement should hang in a straight line both horizontally and vertically—and then you can "go off" a bit within that framework.

Don't spread out all over the place. Keep items close enough that the eye can encompass them all in one pleasing glance. If there's too much space between, the effect will be an explosion that your eye will have to *work* to put together—and that's neither aesthetically pleasing nor relaxing. On the other hand, be careful not to cram items together so that no one item gets the attention it deserves. As I've said, hanging items no more than approximately half their diameter apart is a good rule of thumb to follow—and keep this distance generally uniform throughout (yes, you can variate a bit here and there, as long as your whole arrangement remains in perspective).

Use a variety of shapes and sizes. Combine circles, squares, rectangles—and things both large and small. Use them all in the same wall arrangement, but mix them up: Don't keep small or square or circular items side by side in a grouping, rather, sprinkle them throughout your entire display.

Hang items of three dimensions. Use pictures, mirrors, and plaques whose frames aren't flat against the wall but are contoured or textured. Better yet, use items in your wall arrangements that are a real change of pace such as sconces or hanging figurines, small shelves, or other artistic items. A pair of china birds in flight is a favorite belonging of mine. When something like this is added to an arrangement, it dispels the monotony of more conventional wall treatments—and makes an especially interesting and alive wall combination.

Don't let certain items overpower. If you're displaying heavy frames or dark and ornate items along with more delicate, lighter-colored ones, be sure to strike a balance in your arrangement so that the heavy-darks aren't clumped together while the fragile-light ones look dwarfed. Keep the whole look of your items well balanced and integrated—perhaps putting two heavier oil paintings or sconces with a Spanish look on the ends of your wall grouping, with watercolors and some simpler plaques in between.

Use room accessories in your wall display. If a lamp or plant or even a flower arrangement juts up into the wall area you're working on, place

YES

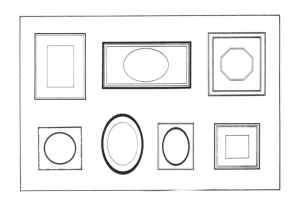

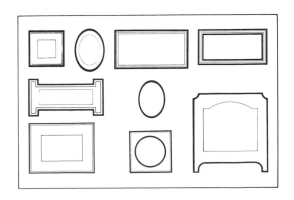

Accessories are a vital part of decorating. These special touches are yours alone and should reflect your own decorating personality.

The accessories illustrated here from *Home Interiors and Gifts* offer a wide selection. The components can be used individually or in groupings.

the hangings around it as though the plant or lamp is *part* of your wall grouping (and therefore part of the balance and unity of your arrangement). In any event, your wall arrangement and your furniture or other room accessories should never fight each other for attention, and one certainly shouldn't be jammed on top of the other.

Don't Overlook Any Areas

Too often people devote their attention to one wall or two, and somehow think the other walls in the room can remain bare. But you need something on *all* walls, so your room won't appear off center or askew.

There are other areas that shouldn't be ignored. What about walls in kitchens, bathrooms, even "mud rooms" where children yank off their boots and washing machine and dryer churn? What about walls in foyers, entryways, halls, and along staircases? All these walls, too, deserve your consideration and provide a wonderful display area for accessories and wall groupings. So check every room or passageway in your house or apartment for empty or lackadaisical walls just waiting to be filled or enlivened.

Don't ignore "secret corners." There are all sorts of nooks and crannies that can hold a picture, plaque, or figurine. I call these bits and pieces of wall "hidden walls," and all it takes is a little imagination to find them. Here's a for instance: Sit down on a chair or sofa and look around. Look at that lamp on an ad-

joining end table. Between the bottom of the lampshade and the top of the table, what do you see? A bit of wall! Another area that you can decorate with accessories, another place where you can add an item to bring additional depth and sustain interest. This new bit of wall is a bonus wall, just waiting for you to accessorize it. It's touches like this that make a winning room—which in turn makes you look good and imparts a very personal touch.

Make much of your mantel. Sometimes that means by not doing *too* much. The accessories you array there shouldn't look too skimpy or too overpowering and should call attention to the wall as a whole rather than to the mantel itself. It's possible, by the way, to give your fireplace a face-lift by creating new facades from materials that are available in most hardware and construction-supply stores. You can add new ceramic tiles or new paneling to give an old fireplace a streamlined contemporary look. Or you can surround it with mirrored panels, so that it stands in a wall of reflected light. Other touches: colorful tiles with Mexican-Spanish designs or old-fashioned Pennsylvania Dutch patterns set around the fireplace opening or across the top of the mantel itself.

Think Themes

Follow a decorating theme or tell a story in your wall grouping. Here's an example. If your theme is Oriental, over your sofa you might hang an

Oriental screen (or a set of fans, or Chinese figurines on a shelf) whose colors are coordinated with the ginger-jar lamps or red lacquered end tables or any such Chinese or Japanese furnishings or accessories throughout the room. If your theme is Victorian, you might hang a what-not shelf holding figurines of an old-fashioned couple—whose clothes pick up on some of the colors in the chintz pillows on your sofa.

Obviously the ideas go on and on, using shelves and plaques and planters to focus and enliven everything from a fairy-tale theme (in a child's room) to a great-outdoors theme for the room of a man or older boy. Imagine a wall relief of a ship, plus a shelf to hold intriguing seafaring items such as seashells or a compass or barometer—all picking up on a boat-wheel headboard and cheery curtains in a nautical pattern.

This sort of thematic approach is such fun—and yet so often people fail to even think of it. They put whatever comes into their heads—and their hands—onto their walls without ever considering the adventure and satisfaction of assembling items that make a statement and bring delight to the people who live or visit within those four walls.

Cottage Garden/Cottage Check copyright © Katzenbach & Warren, Inc.

Little Gems That Make
the Big Difference

Accessories! They're the finishing touches, the jewels of the home. Without them, the most "put together" room looks flat, the most expensively arrayed room looks boring and dull. Just think about rooms you've most admired in the homes of others, in pictures in books and magazines. What gives them their special flair, their unique and welcoming personality, that extra bit of something that makes you smile and want to know the people who live there? It's the pictures and books and plants and pillows, the figurines and flowers and knickknacks and candles that bring everything together and create . . . attraction power!

These extras are to a room what jewelry or scarves or belts are to an outfit. In fact, I think of a room as having a "wardrobe of accessories." Even more, they're often the aesthetic touches we *need* to survive. In the world of nature, so often man comes along and cuts down the trees and paves over the grass and flowers—and then wonders why something is "missing" from his life. That's why it's so important for us to array the insides of our homes with beautiful things that feed our aesthetic and spiritual natures. And picking these accessories gives us a real chance to flex our creative muscles. Decorating is entertaining the eye, and placing the right accessories is like adding the finishing notes to a musical composition or brush strokes to a picture.

There are two basic kinds of accessories: *functional* ones that serve a useful purpose, such as mirrors, candles, or clocks; and *decorative* ones that simply look pretty, such as pictures or plaques or figurines. In either case, accessories deserve to be selected as carefully as any piece of furniture in your home. When selecting accessories, keep in mind these suggestions.

Choosing Your Accessories

Take things personally. Pick what brings you pleasure, what brings a twinkle to your eye, what makes your children smile, what makes your spouse give a low whistle and say, "Hey, I like that." Pick objects that reflect your interests and those of your family, that show off hobbies or skills or family history. Pick objects that *mean something* to you and those you love.

Display your family proudly. Children's artwork or crafts can be framed or boxed or put in Lucite, and nothing makes youngsters prouder than to see their work lovingly shown off. If someone plays an instrument or is proud of special old tools or kitchen equipment or keepsakes, hang the items up or put them out for all to see.

On vacation, have you gathered shells or stones or pine cones? Does your son have a dazzling bag of marbles? Put them out in glass bowls or brandy snifters or small woven baskets. Do you like to knit or do needlepoint? A basket of gloriously colored skeins of wool would look lovely tucked alongside a chair in bedroom or living room. What do the people you live with collect? Angels, bells, miniature elephants, tiny unicorns, or hobby horses? All—or a few carefully chosen pieces—of a collection can add a touch of wonder and scintillation to a room.

Perhaps you're a traveler and have picked up memorabilia from your trips. Perhaps you're a golf enthusiast, or your family likes to skate or ski or boat. Whatever you and your family like to do or watch, let others know by artfully displaying your paraphernalia. You can turn an average room into a terrific room by using items that really mean something to you.

Books could be called a collection, too, and it's always marvelous to see them standing at attention on shelves and in bookcases. Handsome or whimsical bookends can help to hold things up; and if there's room, anything from a figurine to a chunk of coral can add interest. And it goes without saying that an old family Bible—or any Bible—adds a very special note to any room.

Framing your family. There was a time when personal pictures and photographs were deemed suitable only for the bedroom. But believe me, that's no more. If you incorporate photographs into your room—any room—by using good-looking frames arranged on a wall or tabletop, they can enhance it greatly. And speaking of frames, search out mellowed antique ones, or lacquered new ones, or cover worn-out or cardboard ones with fabric that fits with your decor. Another nice touch: Cover the mats inside the frame with fabric, or place those old photos or greeting cards or mementos on a fabric background. For a grouping of pictures or keepsakes, use different but complementary fabrics for a colorful, charming arrangement.

Definitely figure on figurines. Delightful and decorative models of people, animals, birds, and flowers add a touch of life and style to any tabletop or shelf. If you are using a pair, elevate one of the figures to give the pair a more dramatic appearance and allow both to be seen to best advantage.

What to put with figurines? Display silk flowers in an accent color that you wish to bring out in the room. Or array bits of greenery—small ferns or a bit of philodendron—around figurines to give them extra appeal. Or place them alongside dish gardens or terrariums. Or

array with boxes or shells or other treasures.

If you're using objects that may seem unrelated in theme or material, turn them into a complete composition by arranging them on a mat or tray.

A special "through the looking glass" trick: Arrange figurines on mirrors. Add a candle or candles on the mirror, too—and at night when you light them, the effect will be enchanting.

Remember that here, too, as with all your arrangements, a grouping that's symmetrical or all on one level will soon seem static and uninteresting. Arrange figurines, candles, plants so that they're of different heights or on different levels.

Some other treasures that are attractive. There are many items that can be incorporated into your color schemes and room settings, making important contributions for additional color.

Boxes can be both functional and decorative. They may hold (depending on the room they're in) letters and cards, candy, paper clips, pills, tissues—or they may simply sit there and shine handsomely or snap with color.

Canisters provide touches of cheer in kitchens or bathrooms, as well as other areas of the house where they're simply holding whatever you want to put in them.

Baskets can be woven, wicker, metal, or plastic. And they can hold pine cones, skeins of wool, fruit or flowers, magazines, or matchbooks.

Bowls can hold candies, marbles,

The illuminated cabinet displays a collection of wood carvings. These prized
possessions are the "gems that make
the difference."

Accessories in this dining room are eclectic. The centerpiece, a flower arrangement secured in a section of sod, adds a delightful and informal touch to the classic lines of the china and stemware. Candles, as always, provide the glow.

seashells—whatever catches your fancy or reflects your life-style. Bottles, teapots, compote dishes, cups, vases—all can provide that glint of color needed, or pick up on those accent colors you want to emphasize.

Crystal is always classy. Whether in goblets, decanters, vases, or dishes, it's safe to use in any setting.

It goes on and on, according to what catches *your* eye. Paperweights, saucers and plates, goblets and decanters, soap dishes, ashtrays—all can pick up the color scheme in your room and add that extra "twinkle."

Take inventory. Check your basement, attic, even old scrapbooks for forgotten items you could be using— colorful old quilts, turn-of-the-century magazine covers (which look charming in pretty frames), a vase or ashtray or lamp that you got as a present years ago and never knew how to use. Your own home can be the source of many lovely accessories.

Hunt for hardware. Always be on the lookout for those special pieces that make elegant additions to doors, walls, drawers. It's possible to find marvelous door knockers, drawer pulls, doorknobs, plates for light switches—at flea markets, antique or hardware stores, in catalogues—and install them for that magic touch that means so much.

A little about lamps. They light up your life and give rooms a glow that casts an enchanting spell. But be practical and make sure your lamps really do illuminate the areas you in-

tend them for. Sink down on your sofa, plop down in the den, stand in your kitchen, check your children's desks, and *see*—is the lamp you like the look of doing its job and giving people enough light to see/read/cook/study by? Is it placed in such a way that it's of service? Is it placed too high or too low for maximum efficiency; is it casting a glare that will be annoying?

In addition, track lighting or spotlights and floodlights can be added to show off special objects or areas of your room. Is there a special picture or plaque that you adore? What about that enchanting grouping of figurines? Slip a little spotlight on that.

Keep lamps standard size and uncluttered. If you notice a lamp as soon as you come into the room, it's probably a monstrosity—huge and clunky or all covered with "gingerbread." You'll always be safe if you pick lamps with bases that are the classic columns, cylinders, urns, or vases, with sleek and uncomplicated shades.

The enchantment of candles. Candles create a glow that transforms any room with a soft shimmer. Under electric light, you're *eating,* but when there's candlelight, you're *dining.* In addition, candlelight is the best cosmetic. Everyone looks better in candlelight!

Here are some tips for using candles to best advantage:

• Keep them in the refrigerator until ready to use. They'll burn longer.

• Through successive burnings,

keep wick in center of candle and pluck any foreign particles out of the wax. Also, pour off any molten wax building up around wick, otherwise the flame will dwindle almost to nothing and smoking may result.

• Before putting a candle in a cup or container, put a small amount of cooking oil in the bottom. That will help removal of the candle stub when necessary.

• Never put out new, unlit candles with a white wick. Always light that wick, even for a moment, so it's always darkened and burnt.

• Use candles in striking centerpieces. Fill a ceramic bowl with lemons, insert a thick white candle in the center. Or do this with candles of many different colors tucked among many different kinds of fruit—oranges, apples, pears, mangoes.

• Set a multitude of little votive candles on trays, in huge ashtrays, on cake stands, in and on anything that's not flammable. Light them all for a little galaxy of sparkling light.

• Set candles firmly in their holders, then place them directly on a mirror and light up for a Milky Way of magic.

• Place sconces and candleholders in such a way that when the candles are lit, they'll be reflected in mirrors around your home. The more reflection, the more magic you'll create.

The charm of centerpieces. What an easy and inexpensive way to add delight to a dining table or coffee table.

Back to candlesticks again. Take all the candlesticks you own and group them in varying heights in the center of the table. Remove any that

tower too tall and don't allow you to see who's sitting on the other side; but light the others for a shining, central display.

Take a chunk of sod out of a corner of your yard or the woods, place it in a basket or on a platter, and stick in some cut flowers (this casually done arrangement is especially appealing in the spring, when made with crocuses and freesias and hyacinths). Again, keep this all low enough so everyone can see *over* it.

Anything you've got available can be an attractive centerpiece, as well as a conversation piece. What season is it? At Christmas, use a bowl of sparkling ornaments, even a bowl full of twinkling tinsel. At Easter array eggs, or arrange a packed-full bunny basket. At other times, why not a centerpiece of seashells (candles would look good among these too). Or paper fans or origami animals or rolls of ribbon or . . . whatever you've got around.

Try bottles. Many things you buy in the supermarket nowadays come in unusual and attractive bottles in a variety of shapes and sizes—mineral water, mustard jars, soft drinks. Group four or five different bottles and put the same flower or a different flower in each. Beakers, flasks, anything that holds flowers is good. Just make a cluster and center them; add a drop of food coloring to the water for an offbeat accent.

Or use a single flower and float it in a snifter or glass bowl. Or put black rocks—or marbles or pebbles or seashells or pretty gravel (the kind you can buy in the dime store or florist shop)—in the bottom of a bowl

The scrubbable wall covering and the coordinating blue and white checked gingham with its adhesive counterpart effectively and inexpensively create a cheery nursery (*opposite page*).

Colors run rampant in this riotous array of pillows. The theme here is Mexican, but another can be implemented in the same way (*above*).

These canisters, bottles, and copper pieces combine well with the flowers to make a charmingly rustic arrangement against the brick wall (*left*).

and anchor a single flower (or several) in it.

Baskets can take their place on any table, too. Put in several small potted plants, either green or flowering, and center them among plates and silver. It's also charming to flank your main basket with some smaller ones—or to go with several smaller ones to begin with.

Tuck in figurines. It's fun to add figures of birds and animals among your greenery as though they're nestling there.

Make a centerpiece you can eat. Take any vegetable or fruit with firm flesh such as a pumpkin, pear, avocado, or winter squash and hollow out a place for a glass test tube (you can pick them up at medical supply stores). Push the tube into the fruit gently and add flowers that fit.

Here's another happy idea, especially for summer and outdoor eating. Cut horizontally across a watermelon, and make a "basket" centerpiece filled with bright melon balls, crisp mint leaves, and gay, clownlike zinnias. If it's evening, tuck in some tall, slim tapers.

Express yourself by sewing. Whether you have a sewing machine to do some simple running hems or stitches, or want to "sculpt" your environment by sewing by hand with needle and thread, there are many imaginative touches you can add to your surroundings.

Curtains can be made in the styles, colors, and sizes you want by following simple directions in booklets available in most sewing stores or departments. You can buy shirring tapes, rickrack to use for tiebacks, any number of items that help you whip up traditional curtains that drape gracefully or jaunty cafe curtains. You can even make cafe curtains from pretty dishtowels or napkins.

Tablecloths always add a special splash of color, and you can make them yourself with an expanse of a favorite fabric. Another winning idea is to whip up a tablecloth for a round table from a pretty sheet: Measure the diameter of your round tabletop; then add to that the measurement from your table edge to as far as you want the cloth to reach and double that number; then add two inches for a hem. The figure you've now got will be the total diameter of your tablecloth. Next take your sheet, fold it in half from right to left, then from top to bottom (so you've got a sheet that's quartered). Make a "compass" by attaching a string measured to the length of *half* that total diameter to a pencil, and pin the string to the upper right hand corner (or what will be the center of your cloth). Swing that pencil compass down and around in an arc, cut the sheet on the line you've drawn, unfold, and hem by hand or machine. Press the sheet—and you've got a charming tablecloth for dining or display of pictures or accessories.

Cover lampshades by first making a pattern by wrapping brown paper around the existing shade and determining the shade's dimensions. Put this pattern on your fabric, allow about an inch all around for overlaps, and cut out. Then brush white glue evenly all over shade, and when glue becomes tacky, start at back seam and apply your fabric, smoothing as you go. Tuck in edges and seam at overlap and cover edges with rickrack if you wish. It's an easy way to give rooms a special, glowing look. Use the same or matching fabric (or sheets) that you've also used for curtains, tablecloths, napkins, place mats, pillows, spreads, or wallcoverings.

Keep on covering. There are any number of fabrics (quilted ones, too) and edgings and tapes and cording available that will help you cover bed headboards, director's chairs, desk tops—and on and on.

What about covering your kitchen chairs in a fabric that matches your kitchen draperies? And if there's enough material, you could stitch up some napkins or cover some droopy-looking potholders for a more attractive display.

Do you have throw pillows that are a pale shadow of their former selves? Pull a cover-up and stitch them into bright new "wrappings." Or get the basic pillow forms from a department or craft store and introduce brand new cushions into your bedroom or rec room. Here again, the trick up your sleeve is to choose fabrics that complement or coordinate with draperies, wallpaper, and other patterns and colors in your decor.

Now that we have some idea of the wide variety of choices from which to assemble our "wardrobe of accessories," let's consider how to use these pieces to dress up our rooms.

Accessories–Adding
the Finishing Touch

I'm endlessly excited about the use of colorful and charming objects to enhance a room—to give it character and warmth and interest. So it always surprises me when some people just strew accessories about or toss them into a room without thought. Or pop them in as an afterthought because they "think they need something there." Well, they *do* need something there—but it shouldn't be any old thing without personal meaning or expression.

Be careful not to treat your selection of accessories as small odds and ends to fill empty spaces. Your pictures and plaques and figurines and candles are *not* just "filler." They should be coordinated and supply the same indispensable finishing touches to your room that scarves and belts and jewelry do to a clothing ensemble. With accessories, you can add mood, create focal centers of interest, and give unity and balance to the overall look of a room. Properly placed, accessories contribute an important part of the room's "rhythm"; with accessories you can establish a variety in texture, color, and period that you could not accomplish with the other furnishings in the room.

People often read of these ideas, but somehow hesitate to turn them into reality. They have what I call an "Apple Pie House." Did you ever notice how the choice of words on a menu can excite your appetite? The restaurants that attract the most customers never just say "Apple Pie" on the menu, they say "Crusty, Rich, Deep-Dish Apple Pie" or "Spicy Fresh Succulent Apple Pie." Doesn't that *sound* more inviting?

It's the same with our homes. You don't need to have a complicated "recipe" using sophisticated decorating theories. You just need a tried and true recipe with just a touch of "spice"—just a fascinating little something extra like an exotic Indian brass pitcher holding a single rosebud on your coffee table. Or any of the imaginative arrangements we've mentioned. The only difference between a "model house" and a "house that is a model" is that little spice of accessories. Accessories are to the home what spice is to the apple pie! Our homes must satisfy the emotional and psychological needs of our families as well as the physical need of a roof overhead.

What Should Accessories Add?

Color. This is probably the single most important decorating tool, yet the least expensive. So choose accessories in hues and shades and tints that go with your color harmonies, or provide a brilliant or delightful accent to them.

Texture or pattern in pillows or end tables or baskets or boxes adds the excitement of contrast. Wicker "feels" rough, both to the touch and to the eye; glass feels—and looks—smooth; fabrics feel and appear soft . . . or nubby, or silky, or woolly.

Form brings variety to a room. Figurines, flowers, pictures, shelves—all have different forms, which add interest to your surroundings. Instead of a room being only linear or geometric, it can have a range of shapes that captures your eye and makes things come alive.

Balance is achieved when you place accessories in such a way that they even out all your other elements. So you've got a big, comfy chair on one side of the room, and don't really have another large piece of furniture to juxtapose against it. Well, add a stocky but fairly tall plant on the other side of the room. Or plop some king-size pudgy cushions over there on the floor. Or maybe an end table displaying an arrangement of tall candles would round out the room in such a way that no one element in it seems too heavy.

Elements to Consider in Accessorizing a Room

Line means the eye is led to the center of interest or focal point of the room by the arrangement of accessories. Be careful not to group all your items in one corner of the room or in such a way that attention is drawn away from your main conversation area or the part of the room you'd like to emphasize.

Shape refers to the arrangement of a room. In symmetrical arrangement everything is evenly balanced in a formal or traditional way. When an arrangement is asymmetrical, however, things are more informal and relaxed; it gives a room a fresh, young approach that many people today enjoy and appreciate.

Space enhances the effect of the accessories by allowing the eye room to roam and enjoy the completed look of the whole. If you've crowded items on top of each other so there's no breathing room, you and visitors alike will have that claustrophobic feeling.

Scale refers to the relationship of accessories to each other within a room. An enormous vase or towering lamp shouldn't be allowed to dwarf all other items alongside it. If your candleholders or figurines are large, don't put them on a table with tiny little boxes or miniature items. Keep all elements "in step" with one another so no one takes over and gets *all* the attention.

Unity and harmony means that each group of accessories seems correct and belongs together to create a total look. A fragile china bowl full of blown-out and painted Easter eggs just doesn't fit with a heavy metal letter opener on a high-tech chrome table.

If your accessories have *rhythm,* your eye will flow right along over them; the repetition of shape, theme, color, and pattern will all blend together in a pleasing way.

Being aware of all these factors may sound intimidating. Believe me, it's not! All these are things your eye—and common sense—will begin to pick up naturally as you become more and more attuned to their presence and importance. Soon elements of scale and harmony and balance will seem like second nature to you—and you will automatically take them into account as you survey and rearrange all your accessories around you. Not only that—it will be creative fun!

Arranging Your Accessories

Make a clean sweep. Just as your eye reads from left to right, it also moves left to right when surveying a room. Keep that in mind as you add your objects, and stand back to look yourself—if your eye stops at something that's jarring, it's out of place.

Support one focal point. Every room should have one interesting architectural feature or point of interest around which everything else is grouped. This might be a fireplace or dining room table or a coffee table

This cozy room with its coordinated accessories invites guests to "Come on in
and sit a spell."

Fresh flowers artfully arranged in this
earthenware crock strike a cheery note.
Strawberries demand to be sampled,
and the fragrance of the fruit permeates
the setting.

Here is another example of how clev-
erly food and flowers can be presented.
The hollowed-out squash with its scal-
loped edge serves as a compote for the
vegetables while the pumpkin becomes
a vessel for seasonal flowers.

that acts as the center of a furniture grouping. Keep in mind that accessories should complement this scheme as well.

Make your own compositions— on end tables, coffee table tops, shelves. Interesting arrangements are created by using objects of different shapes and heights. One guideline is to have objects of three different heights—high, medium, and low. For example: a taller lamp, a medium-height plant, and a low candy box; a tall candlestick, a bouquet of daisies, and a splendid old paperweight. Here's still another possibility: a tall spray of gladiola in a vase, a pair of figurines about nine inches high, and a handsome old leather-bound book.

Sometimes, though, everything is low. It can be quite dramatic or delightful to have several small objects on a tabletop, and in that case there's greater impact in the common theme. You might assemble a collection of enameled boxes, some fluted seashells, a grouping of brass candlesticks with candles.

Leave enough space between accessories so each piece can be shown off to best advantage. And yet don't spread things out so much that an item stands alone on an expanse of boring wall or tabletop.

Keep your balance. Here too, as in all of decorating, certain elements of color, size, scale, and balance must be kept in mind when accessorizing a room. You can't toss in a pillow that's wildly out of whack with your color scheme, hang only one tiny picture over a huge overstuffed sofa, or put a fragile china shepherdess in a room that's otherwise modern and bold.

Be careful of overkill. A room jammed with everything under the sun will certainly look too cluttered. On the other hand, a room with too few accessories will look unfinished—and just plain not as pretty. Try to hit a happy medium.

Consider child proofing. Keep in mind the ages of those who come visiting. If toddlers are toddling on your premises, keep your delicate crystal up high and your velvet cushions in storage for a later time. Instead, display objects that are sturdy enough so your heart won't sink whenever a child is in the room.

Be marvelous to your mantel. It's often the room's focal point, so decorate this area with care. It is probably the place to hang your most stunning painting or dramatic three-dimensional figures. Many decorators will tell you to keep the rest of the mantel surface uncluttered so as not to detract from the painting or clock or sculpture hung there, and I suppose this is good advice if you can follow it. But many mantels seem to end up collecting any number of charming figures or other treasures—and I say if these are things you love dearly, go ahead and enjoy them.

Foliage, figurines, brass collections, candlesticks look great on mantels. Use pairs—a pair of figurines, a pair of boxes, a pair of candlesticks—displayed as sets on both ends of the mantel to give a feeling of balance.

Include Your Whole House

Accessories aren't just for the living or dining room. They belong in every room, whether it's the bathroom or kitchen, even basement or garage (a charming little plaque or mirror hung up over a workbench or light switch can bring a smile—or a chuckle—to anyone, whatever he or she is doing, and add personality to an otherwise neglected area). And don't forget those rooms that aren't quite rooms, such as the entryway or hallway or "funny little corner."

Include the whole family. Ask youngsters, teens, maybe older family members who might be living with you to help pick out accessories that appeal to them, to get in on the act of making their surroundings more pleasant. Draw everybody in, expand your thinking to encompass every nook and cranny, every kid and granny.

Salute the Seasons

Mother Nature changes her accessories four times a year, and we should be able to change ours at least twice a year. You wouldn't think of confining yourself to one set of earrings, would you? Well, accessories are the jewels of the home, and they too take on new sparkle and zest when they are changed around. Many times by wise shopping you can find accessories that have great versatility and can be used in every room in your home, taking on a new look in each grouping.

Change accessories to give your home a different look for summer and winter—even spring and fall. It will give rooms a fresh look that will brighten everyone's spirits and give all a new perspective. In the fall bring out the bronzes and brasses, gleaming copper candleholders, figurines in colors of rust, burgundy, and chocolate, items of wood and flowers like chrysanthemums, pillows of heartier velvet and nubbier textures. As spring breezes drift in and summer's softness tantalizes, change to more fragile figurines, touches of wicker, curtains of gauze, pictures that sing of the season, pillows of chintz and seersucker.

Although it is not always possible, some people even change furniture, switching an overstuffed armchair for a rocker of white wicker. Or removing cozy winter slipcovers for sunny cotton ones. Another way to make the swing of seasons fun: Bring out a treasured object only at certain times of the year. For instance, *Home Interiors* has a figurine called Bunny Love that would be perfect for an appearance on a coffee table in the spring, only to go back into its storage "hutch" in the fall. This way, just as beloved Christmas ornaments are brought forth to oohs and ahs in December, certain objects can be brought out to signal the change in seasons and be enjoyed from a fresh perspective.

Something About Scents

The things you *see* aren't the only part of decorating. What you smell is important, too. Leave bowls of cut tart lemons or luscious oranges in a room and let the bracing scents bring

Rose Bower/Summer Arbor copyright © Katzenbach & Warren, Inc.

The warmth of wood, the earth tones in
the color scheme, and the coordinating
accessories invite one to sit a spell,
enjoy a cup of tea, or read or muse in
this homey atmosphere (*left*).

A sea anemone rests at a lamp base,
and seashells combine with an enameled bowl and porcelain vase to present
an interesting mix of accessories on this
skirted table. The white of the wrought
iron mirror frame, the wicker container,
and the painted brick of the fireplace
unifies the mixture of furnishings
(*above*)

smiles to everyone's face. Vanilla is another elixir to splash on light bulbs or dot around a room. Clove-studded oranges create an appealing aroma as well (and these too could make one of those centerpieces we just mentioned).

Create your own flower *potpourri.* Rose petals work wonderfully, but nearly any flowers will do (and a mix is really nice). Gently pull off petals (in early morning if you can), spread on paper in a protected place where breezes won't scatter them and sun won't fade them, and turn daily so they dry evenly. After three or four days, petals are ready to go into jars or bowls or boxes. If you want to add even more aroma, moisten a cotton ball with some fragrant bath oil or one of the "essential oils" you can buy at pharmacies or herb stores, and tuck it into the mixture.

Make simple sachets by taking cotton balls moistened with the bath or essential oils and bundling them up with other cotton balls in a lacy hanky or napkin or bit of pretty material. Fasten it all up with a bit of ribbon, and place in areas where a dash of fragrance will always be welcome—in drawers or closets or even out among other belongings in main rooms.

What Accessories Go With "Your" Furniture Period?

The rustic, hardy appeal of *Early American* calls for more informal accessories made from pine, maple, oak, or finishes simulating these woods. Also appropriate would be objects with the look of copper, or some simpler hammered or wrought iron pieces. Plaques or clocks with the traditionally popular "innkeeper sign" shapes are always favorites; so are plaques or pictures showing game birds, animals, pioneer men and women, or country scenes. Most objects that go well with Early American decor have a flat rather than a shiny look. Warm colors are right, too.

If your home has the more formal flavor of a more prosperous colonial period—say, *Eighteenth Century English*—then avoid rustic accessories. Suitable for you are picture frames with gold finishes, porcelain, glass, and more delicate silvers. The shinier or softly glowing finishes are excellent for your surroundings. Specific accessories that would be right for your room: mirrors with eagles centered at the top, items that remind you of the early days of our country without going back quite to the colonists. Brass, by the way, goes with all periods. Brass is to a room what a smile is to your face.

French Provincial is neither as rustic as Early American nor as formal as Eighteenth Century English. Look for accessories that suit an informal yet sophisticated way of life—plaques showing weathervanes, trees, and flowers, mirrors with floral carvings and latticework designs, objects of pewter and china. Dried flowers are especially good in these settings, too.

Many different types of accessories fit in with the romantic, substantial look of furniture adapted from *Spanish* and *Mexican* styles. Oak and iron objects that are bold, somewhat daring and overscaled, add to the charm of the *Mediterranean* mood. Gold and black are good colors to use, too. Since Mediterranean is a flexible style that allows a lot of latitude, be imaginative. Any choices you make will probably be right if you stay away from anything too delicate in scale.

Many people today adore *Victorian* furnishings, and the accessories used here should be more delicate and whimsical—bulky, earthy pieces won't do. Look for demure figurines with a more fragile look, mirrors with delicate filigree, sconces that look "shy" rather than hearty, colors that blush rather than burst with vigor. Pieces of crystal, china plates in pastel colors, lamps with lacy shades—they'll all be right.

Six Necessary Ingredients

I'm going to close this chapter with the Six Necessary Ingredients for accessorizing a room. Every room needs a touch of *black* for drama; a touch of *wood* for warmth; the gleam of *brass* for light; the glow of *candlelight* for atmosphere; flashes of *white* to tie everything together with unity; the green of *plants* and *flowers* for freshness. With all these elements, any room will sing. And call out, "Come inside!"

And now more about those flowers and plants coming up in the next chapter.

Wisteria and Sparrow©, Wisteria and Sparrow Border©, Stephanie Companion, E. C. Carter Sheer, copyright Greeff Fabrics, Inc.

Adding Lovely Life
With Flowers and Plants

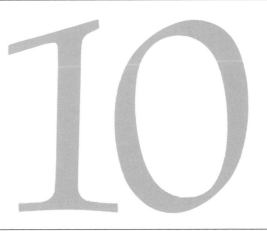

Flowers and plants always add a fresh and special look that can't be duplicated. After all, Solomon in all his glory was not arrayed as one of these. Whether you're using "lilies of the field" in a vase on a coffee table, or adding a tumble of Swedish ivy to an end table, or slipping a spray of silk flowers into a corner, these beautiful additions add life to every part of your home.

Amazing imposters. Before getting to the "real thing," I'd like to let you know the latest about some flowers and plants that aren't quite what they seem. Today there are many lovely flowers made of silk or fabric or even polyethylene plastic that either look real—or are facsimiles that are equally attractive. Such flowers aren't meant to replace the beauties from your garden, but to add to the blossoms that may be available from your summertime cuttings. Plastic or silk flowers last through all seasons, are practical to keep and care for— and today come in versions that look absolutely real or elegant or striking . . . or just plain pretty.

Flowers clean up easily—silk and silk-look flowers may be cleaned by gently "brushing" them with a feather duster or by using a blow dryer set on low and cool to blow dust off. If more heavily soiled, wet a clean cloth in mild, soapy water and gently wipe off the petals. Treat your lovely silk flowers as you would a fine fabric—which they are! Flowers made of polyethylene plastic can be sprayed with hair spray; as the hair spray evaporates, so does the dust. If more heavy-duty cleaning is required for plastic flowers, just dip in a mild solution of soapy ammonia and water (don't use a cleaner that has an oily base).

Beauteous blossoms. Snip flowers right out of your own garden. The best time to do this is in the early morning, very late afternoon, or early evening when it's coolest. At these times of day the blossoms won't be droopy with the heat, and won't respond by wilting minutes after being taken into the house.

Remember that a bouquet can consist of a single flower as well as an armful. When you use flowers, remember that light and shadow can play a part in your decorating scheme as well. Arrange flowers in places where the natural sunlight streams in to cast dappled shadows, or where your lighting fixtures throw patterns of dark and light as well.

Give flowers plenty of room between each other. Just like people, they need room for air to circulate around them, to cool them and give them space to "breathe." Flowers crammed together in a vase too small for them will make you feel crowded and hot, too.

Don't forget that wild flowers and roadside flowers also make striking arrangements. Gather tall beach grasses, cattails, wheat, anything you see that strikes you as pretty (and doesn't make people sneeze). Or swing to the opposite extreme and float one exquisite water lily (or gardenia or rose) in a bowl.

Outstanding arrangements. Whether your flowers are live or made of other materials, here are some tips for making the most striking arrangements.

In a flower grouping, keep light colors and buds on the top or at the outer edges of your arrangement. Darker colors and partially opened flowers and buds come next, in the "middle." And the darkest colors and fully opened flowers should be at the center of the grouping, at the heart where they'll act as a focal point. A good combination is to use, say, five flowers of one lighter color, three of a color that's a bit darker, and only one of the darkest color, which will go as an accent at the center of your grouping. If you are working out such an arrangement, remember that odd numbers are better than even ones for good composition.

Use different heights of flowers and greenery to make things interesting. And use different shapes of flowers—tall spikes of gladiolas with fat, round daisies; graceful spires of larkspur with fluffy carnations and mums. If you don't have tall flowers to combine with shorter, more roly-poly ones, then use two or more colors of flowers for contrast.

White or yellow are both "safe" colors and excellent for all decors. If there's a question in your mind about what "goes" in any setting, remember, one of these two colors is sure to fit in any color scheme.

How large should an arrangement be? Most designers agree that it looks best if the arrangement is one to one and one-half times the width or the height of the container. And what container? As long as it holds water, anything goes: a bucket or basin, a teapot or salad bowl, a basket in which you've tucked a bowl or plastic storage container. Incorporate the color of the container into your design.

Don't ignore the back of an arrangement. Save your odd pieces of flowers and greenery to complete the arrangement on the edges or in back blank spots. Sometimes people take great care to place flowers just so in the front and then put the flowers in front of a mirror where the back of the grouping shows, too! So don't ignore any aspect of what you've assembled.

It's fine to leave some space between flowers around the outside edge of the arrangement; these "voids" keep your flowers from having a crowded look. Spaces in the middle, however, aren't usually desirable—they're just holes! Again, the trick is to make everything blend harmoniously together without seeming crammed.

If you're displaying your arrangement with figurines (sometimes you'll even want to put the figurines *in* your arrangement), use only one or two. Remember, our eyes scan a room or arrangement from left to right, so it's best to keep any figures you display at the right.

Use your imagination in flower arranging. Sit down, spread out your flowers, and create!

What's your flower personality? Some psychologists and scholars think that flowers can provide a clue to a person's personality. Here are some examples:

Orchid lovers are often warm and emotional people who have a flair for the dramatic and are quick to laugh or cry.

Roses are the favorite flower of down-to-earth, practical people.

Violets are usually the favorites of people who pay attention to details and are very orderly or meticulous.

Honeysuckle is often favored by romantics, happy people, and those who like fun.

Daisies and bluebells are the usual choice of individualists, or persons who like change and meeting new people.

People who like big bright flowers such as sunflowers and gladiola are often flamboyant, quick and relaxed talkers, and the most fun at parties.

Plants of varying species and differing heights add a special dimension in the corner grouping (*right*).

The colorful floral centerpiece on the table, the potted geraniums on the terrace, and the greenery make for "lovely life" and relaxed dining in this light and airy room (*below*).

Nature's beauty pervades this modern grouping through live—and spectacular—plantings (*opposite page*).

Some happy talk about house-plants. Houseplants are a graceful, glorious way to hide and soften awkward corners, to perk up dull backgrounds, to divide rooms and hide unsightly areas, to bring a touch of life to "dead" areas and droopy tabletops. There are houseplants for every area of your home—dimly lit entryways, windowsills dazzled with sunlight, kitchen counters, bedroom nooks where only artificial light is present. Here are some ways that plants can be used.

As a room divider. If your room is large, or you want to set off certain places as work areas or conversation nooks, plants can act as an effective room divider that's simply not as harsh or intimidating as an actual wall. Group medium or large-size plants to make a living wall that clearly sets off certain areas without the sterner harshness of a partition. This is an especially good tip for apartment dwellers or people in smaller houses or trailers, where you'd like to divide off areas without making space seem even smaller.

If your room is big, "divide and conquer" with big plants such as rubber trees (*Ficus elastica decora*), Mexican breadfruit (*Monstera deliciosa*), popularly called split-leaf philodendron, or tall and delicately drooping weeping figs (*Ficus benjamina*). And if you make a grouping of these plants, using different textures and sizes, you'll continue to have an airy, open effect that doesn't block or isolate space—but creates a distinct area.

If your room is smaller, separate areas by using more delicate foliage such as Boston or asparagus ferns, or shorter varieties such as lacy tree philodendron (*Philodendron selloum*) or members of the palm family.

To call attention to special details. If you have beams or windows or shelves or closed-off fireplaces that need to be noticed, add a plant that calls out with color—but doesn't overwhelm your area. Suspend a fern or philodendron in a hanging basket, tuck a kangaroo vine (*Cissus antarctica*) over the fireplace.

To balance things out. Sometimes you need "something" in a room to lift your eye, to balance out the grouping of pictures or mirrors you have on one wall. Well, balance things with a stately, tall *Dracaena* or *Monstera deliciosa* (these names may sound a little imposing, but they're really just the botanical names of all those "nice big trees and pretty plants" you see in gardening stores and greenhouses). On the other hand, often the furniture you have and the size of your room calls for a single small plant or two; a piggyback plant (*Tolmiea menziesii*) or a silvery gray leafed watermelon plant (*Peperomia sandersii*) would make an elegant highlight in a smaller space.

Light up your life with bulbs. Here's a fresh and beautiful way to bring color into your home. Look for bulbs such as *clivia* (sparkling orange, yellow, and salmon-colored flowers), *freesias* (delicate, fragrant blossoms that have a scent like the most spectacular day of spring), *tuberous begonias* (what an assortment of dazzling colors these come in!), and *gloxinia* (pastel and almost waxy blooms). And don't overlook the absolutely outstanding blooms of the *amaryllis;* just pot these incredible bulbs and stand back. Day by day you can watch the stem shoot up and huge lilylike flowers of red, white, and orange burst out. These bulbs can be ordered from many catalogues or found in many nurseries or florists' shops.

For a real touch of glamor, try orchids. It's actually easier to grow them than most people think. And then swinging to the opposite extreme of sophistication, in a sunny window it's possible to grow everything from geraniums to morning glories!

Try a terrarium. Put some small pebbles in the bottom of a jar, globe, aquarium—in anything that's clear glass with a lid to close off the top. Sprinkle on bits of charcoal to keep soil sweet, then layer soil on top of that to about a third of the container's depth. Plant any kind of small greenery that fits inside, then add just enough water to make things moist, and cover with the lid.

You can make all sorts of miniature worlds in this way. And place them in any well-lit spot (but not in direct sun) for everyone to enjoy.

Lush touches you can eat. Herbs can be grown inside in a sunny window—then pinched regularly to go into soups, stews, salads. Fragrant *basil* will fill your life with pungent pleasure. So will *rosemary, sage, lemon balm, thyme* and *marjoram, oregano* and *dill.*

If you've got a lot of light, many miniature vegetables can actually be grown indoors, in hanging baskets or windowsill pots. Look for miniature varieties in seed catalogues and gardening centers. Today there are small vegetable varieties from Tom Thumb lettuce (a head of it is about as big as a tennis ball) to corn that's as high as an Airedale's eye). It's tomatoes, though, that most people love to grow, so get Pixie and other midget varieties, and get them growing in your kitchen—or maybe even in the children's room.

What about fabulous fluorescents? If you have dim rooms or corners, or your home or apartment doesn't get much natural sunlight, you can place your plants under artificial lights. Particularly efficient and beneficial to plants are fluorescent lights. They use less energy and can be placed close to tender green leaves without scorching them.

The big drawback used to be that fluorescent lights cast such a cold light that people were reluctant to have them in their homes. But now tubes have been developed that give light that is warmer and more appealing for home use. Many tubes are especially intended for use with plants. Many fluorescent fixtures are available in slim, compact strips that can easily be installed under cabinets, over shelves, wherever you wish.

Cast a pretty shadow. Place floor lamps, "tube" lamps (ones that throw light straight up at the ceiling), or track lights in such a way that when evening comes and the lights go on, plants (and other special accessories too) will be illuminated. A light tucked in a corner by a graceful ficus tree will produce fairyland shadows that will make a room romantic and "foresty." Experiment by placing lamps alongside individual plants or groupings to see what position creates the most appealing play of light and shadow.

Guidelines for good groupings. In entryways, bedrooms, even bathrooms, gather plants together for maximum effect. Combine plants that have similar needs as far as light, watering, and humidity are concerned (you can easily find this out by consulting a gardening book or garden-center attendant). Place taller plants in back, smaller ones in front, and give any plants that need it (or need to be staggered for visual effect) an extra boost by placing them on upside-down pots or whatever is available to give plants a visual lift.

It's a good idea, if possible, to put those plants you have grouped together on a waterproof tray filled with pebbles. This way your floor will be protected—plus, any water that runs off plants and onto the tray will evaporate and give plants that extra bit of humidity they love.

Browse your way to beauty. Just wander around your local nursery or plant store and see what's available in everything from filmy ferns that go on a tabletop to towering trees that take up a whole corner—and find out what the store staff suggests for your home. Or ask friends just what that leafy beauty is sprouting with such vim and vigor in the corner of *their* home. In this way you can pick up what would be right for your particular quarters.

When you buy, be prepared to give the salesman the answers to these questions: How much light do you have in the location where you'll be placing the plant? Is your room excessively hot or cold—or dry or humid? Many plants today come with a stake that gives information you need for making an intelligent choice—and maintaining the plant in the manner to which it has become accustomed.

Every room of your house or apartment can benefit from the freshness of flowers, the prettiness of plants, the glory of greenery. There are endless ways to incorporate these grand and growing things into your decorating scheme. So move plants around, try them in different places, get new bulbs started every six weeks or so, and you'll always have sparkling color as a part of your life, even in the winter. You'll have a home that's not just a home—it's a garden.

Rooms That Grow

As You Do

When do we really start decorating our homes? When do we actually begin developing our ideas about beauty and comfort, about how we want our own homes to look and feel?

I think that it starts very, very early in our lives. My mother died before I was two years old, and I lived with my grandparents on a wheat farm on the rolling plains of Kansas until I was six-and-a-half. My grandparents were dear and godly people, and my earliest memories are of them kneeling beside my bed at night praying for me. A candle burned on the table beside us, and just beyond its gold and quivering light were the walls of the room, my room, where I felt protected and safe. I knew I was loved and cared for, and that a great and kind God watched over us all.

The surroundings of my room, and in all of my grandparents' home, reflected that feeling. Even when his crops were destroyed by hail, my grandfather came in singing, "Have Thine own way, Lord, have Thine own way." I will never forget the feeling of trust and confidence and peace that existed in that house—and the furnishings and fabrics and the pictures on the wall and the items propped on the mantel all seemed unutterably dear to me. I know those first ideas about how a harmonious, happy home should look have stayed with me all my life.

Over the years my ideas and tastes have continued to grow and develop. I've studied and observed and learned as much as I can about the principles of good design. I've visited in homes of beauty, and browsed in museums, and studied the work of fine professionals. I've become more aware and sensitive about all the good ideas that make homes pleasing and warm—and I never intend to stop learning! But those basic ideas about decorating begin way back—and then we just keep adding to them, observing a little here, experimenting a little there. Oh, it's never ending. And it never fails to be fun.

Unfortunately, some people seem to think they're "locked" into a specific style of decorating that they choose at a certain point in their life . . . and should never change. I read recently that a psychologist and a professor of psychiatry at a well-known medical center said that "fear of furnishing" was common among more than 50 percent of the population! He reported that people were so afraid of being "trapped" by their decisions and afraid of "failing" in their decorating choices that they often went through life *never* picking furniture or accessories!

Isn't that a shame? Just think of the pleasure some people miss because they don't trust the common sense and good taste that God gave them! Often as I consult with people I have to remind them that success (in decorating or anything else) isn't something set in stone. Success is a moving target. You never really arrive. You fail a little, you learn a little—and you always keep moving along.

Another thing to remember is that what you consider success when you're twenty or thirty is different from success when you're forty—or fifty or sixty or seventy. Or when you're married, or single, or have children, or have an extended family of relatives and friends.

In other words, your decorating scheme is like anything else in life— it *changes*. So go with it. Say yes to ongoing developments. Let your decorating scheme grow as *you* grow. Here are some of the ways.

In the Beginning

Be realistic about your budget. If this is your first house or apartment, your budget is probably small. So make yourself sit down and figure out how much money you have to spend—and what furnishings and accessories you really *need*. Today some people think they have to have a

The bamboo theme imparts a light, informal look to this dining room grouping. These pieces are part of a versatile
modular collection.

Fabric is a valuable decorating tool. In this easygoing apartment it brightens and unifies a mix of odd pieces of furniture and highlights a window area that might otherwise be nondescript.

fancy this and a modern that to get along. But the fact is we don't need everything at once; a few basic pieces can get us along quite happily.

Set priorities. Spend the most on items that will get the hardest wear and that you expect to last the longest. Invest money in a good mattress or a sturdy sofa instead of in a chic coffee table or an elegant etagere. Concentrate on buying the items that are essential, and leave the others for later.

Invest in one or two quality items rather than numerous cheaper ones. When you're first moving in, it's tempting to buy a lot of items of lesser quality—a bedroom suite, a dinette set, chairs and end tables and a convertible sofa—that aren't quite what you want, but you can't wait. Well, waiting isn't so bad at all. Buy a few well-made and good-looking furnishings, then fill in with castoffs or secondhand or unfinished furnishings until the time comes when you're ready to move on to the next quality addition.

Use your imagination. Your most valuable decorating tool is free of charge—it's your own ingenuity. Keep your eyes open for "finds" in flea markets, import and discount stores, furniture outlets, garage sales, and in the attics of friends and family.

Brush a new, bright coat of paint on some pieces, stain ones that are unfinished, drape cheerful chintz over others. Give castoffs and hand-me-downs a paint pick-me-up—and use these standbys until you and your bank account are ready for the next big decorating move. Then when you can afford to replace these "filler" pieces, move them to another room (by that time you may have a bigger house, or children's rooms to furnish), or sell them at your own garage sale.

Keep a plan in mind. Stay flexible—but be consistent in working toward the look you want. Keep a notebook if necessary, use graph paper to actually map out room arrangements and furniture groupings as you slowly assemble accessories and create an atmosphere. "Slowly" can sometimes mean years, so it's important to remember and stick to the atmosphere you're trying to create. It's possible to become so carried away with a charming Chinese red lacquered chest seen in a department store that you forget it doesn't *go* with those other items you've been assembling for a country look.

Working Toward a Definite Decor

What *are* the elements to keep in mind as you put together a room over weeks, months, or years? Here they are. First choose a decor that delights you (some of the most popular are listed below) and then start putting together the items that will make it come alive.

English Traditional. The feeling is warm and inviting. The colors to use are blue and gold, rose, soft pastels, moss green, and pink. The fabrics to

Here we have additional furniture units from the bamboo-accented modular collection. This versatile furniture can be adapted to the next stage of your decorating life and incorporated into other rooms.

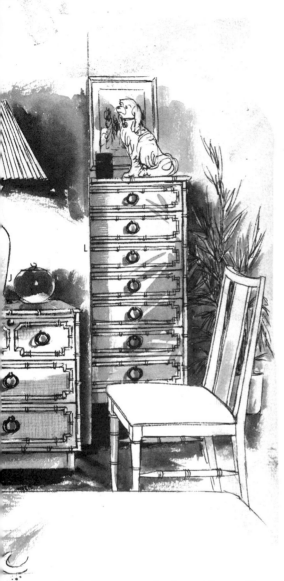

use here are soft oranges, russet reds, golds and browns, greens and Wedgwood blues. Use natural fabrics such as nubby wools and cottons, in plaids, patchwork, and small patterns. Your wood finishes should be maple, pine, or oak, in any of their types and tones from light to dark. Add accessories of brass; antique reproductions of sconces, mirrors, shelves; wooden boxes; woven baskets. Use floral arrangements that are casual and colorful, perhaps made up of gourds and sheaves of wheat, or real vegetables and fruits clustered with greenery.

Oriental. Here's a look and feel that's clean, simple, and comfortable. Blacks and whites add crispness, peaches, reds, blues, and rusts add to the elegant charm. Silks, satins, and cottons go well in rooms like these (cover screens with these fabrics, too). Bamboo finishes look fine; so do lacquered finishes, satiny black woods, various wood inlays. A floral arrangement can be made of a few dramatic stalks or blossoms—a spray of gladiola or orchids, a calla lily or two, a single gerbera daisy . . . perhaps with a single fern or leaf (one spring branch of forsythia or quince would be gorgeous, too). The ideal accessories here are pieces of glinting brass or glowing copper; fans look lovely, too, and simply framed prints and silkscreens go perfectly on the walls.

Modern. The feel you're working toward here is practical and honest, functional and comfortable. The lines and materials seem pure, cool, and

look for are velvets, cottons, linens—and brocades, plaids, chintz, or small formal patterns. The wood finishes that belong here are fruitwood or mahogany in shades light to dark, or pale antique colors. Floral arrangements should be small; ferns and bowls or boxes of potpourri add a beguiling touch. Accessories should be made of crystal or porcelain with gold trim; white antique items with simple lines would be perfect, too.

Country and Colonial. The feeling you want to achieve in these rooms is cheerful and cozy. The colors to new. The colors that create this kind of ambience can range from pales to brights, or can be natural or analogous. Wood finishes can be dark or light; metals and glass fit into this particular picture, too. The accessories you gather should reflect this crisp, sleek look: unadorned mirror and picture frames in metal or teak, pillows in solid colors or bold stripes, vases and pitchers and trays with bold, clean lines. Track lighting is very effective in this sort of setting. And the "lines" everywhere, from furniture to furniture groupings, should be geometric—straight lines, rectangles, even triangles. The floral arrangements that go best in this sort of setting are gay and simple splashes of color—perhaps several vivid tulips or lilies, perhaps a mass of daisies or mums; ferns go well as a back-up to these arrangements, or as an ensemble in their own right.

Eclectic. This wonderful lived-in look has become more and more popular. And since eclectic includes different styles and designs of furniture and accessories, this look is obviously a natural one to choose for rooms that you intend to "grow" over the years. Eclectic can mean a little bit of everything, as long as it's in good taste. Such rooms have a feeling of lightness, casualness, ease. The colors to assemble are bright, monochromatic or complementary (or a mixture of both). In eclectic rooms, color can play an especially important part: Since you're assembling different styles and periods of furniture and accessories, the unifying element that brings them all to-

gether is color—on walls or in upholstery fabrics. You can use fabrics in anything from cotton to velvet, in solids or plaids or stripes or florals (almost anything goes except vinyls). Wood finishes can be wood tone, painted woods, natural woods—here again, practically anything. Accessories? The best (or most beloved) of anything you can get your hands on—country, traditional, Oriental, Mediterranean, or English, all can be incorporated into an eclectic decorating scheme. And, oh, the floral arrangements you can put together, everything from masses of wildflowers to a single spray of gladiola, from a bowl of backyard marigolds to a tumble of dried or straw flowers, from chic silk flowers to a china bouquet. It's clear that an eclectic decorating scheme encompasses everything—and can develop easily over the years as your finances and life-style change.

Keep Growing

Whichever of these choices you make, it's never too late (or early) to start assembling the rooms you hope to have—at whatever point in your life. Some people buy new furniture and accessories or slap paint on walls willy-nilly, without any thought about what look they eventually hope to achieve. Whether you're a newlywed, or your family has grown and gone, or you're living alone, or sharing with an extended family— look ahead! And start working toward that homey or exciting atmosphere that *can* be assembled over the weeks or months or years. Here are

In a beginning room such as this, with its unrelated mixture of furnishings, color on the walls and in the fabrics is the unifying element that brings it all together.

some ideas to help the rooms in your apartment or house "grow up" in the same way your budget and your life do.

Pick furnishings that do double duty—and adapt to your life as you go along. If you're starting out in a small home or apartment, invest in furnishings that are flexible and play dual roles. Today sofas, chairs, even hassocks, chests, and wall systems open up into beds; a graceful drop-leaf table can wait closed up along a wall until it's time to open up for company. Bookcases can act as room dividers, or parts of work areas or entertainment areas. Chairs can be scooted around on casters, drawer units can be tucked under and around beds to provide extra storage space.

Modular furniture and sectional pieces are also wonderful choices for beginning decorators and people whose living quarters will be growing and changing. Today these sectional pieces come in both contemporary, squared-off forms as well as more gracefully curving ones—and can be rearranged to give a room a different look. Then, as you add new furnishings over the years, or move to a different home and rooms of a different size, these sectional pieces can be shifted according to your needs.

When you use versatile furniture such as this, you can transform a dining area into a sleeping area, or a work space into a visiting nook—and make good use of every bit of where you live. *And* such furnishings can be adapted to the *next* stage of your decorating life—and moved to other areas or incorporated into other rooms. The same goes for accessories which may start off in the living room of your first home—then later perhaps become part of the decor of a bedroom or den. When you choose quality items that really please you and those you love, they can be a part of your life forever . . . and be moved and changed as *you* move and change.

Fill in with budget beauties— especially in the beginning. Who needs money when you have your imagination? There's no end to the fun and pretty things you can do to

liven up rooms without a lot of cash (and then as your money and space grow, you can replace temporary pieces with higher quality furnishings). Here are some examples.

Get old school lockers or filing cabinets, in secondhand shops or junkyards, and paint them in high-gloss, cheerful colors. Use them for storage; put a piece of plywood or butcher block across two shorter fil-

ing cabinets to make a sturdy desk. Cover metal chairs with bright, glossy colors, too, for playroom or study or dining room or kitchen.

Watch for wicker in flea markets and at garage sales. Give items a fresh coat of paint, and they'll look like a million.

Lamps can be a major purchase. So as you're getting your feet on the ground, use paper lanterns. Suspend

a big one from the ceiling, use a dimmer control to turn things softer, lighter, brighter as you wish. Or go to camera or hardware stores and get simple lights that clamp onto bedposts or sills.

It still is fun to make shelves by layering painted scraps of lumber with cement blocks or bricks. Or if you or a member of your family is handy with a hammer, make some

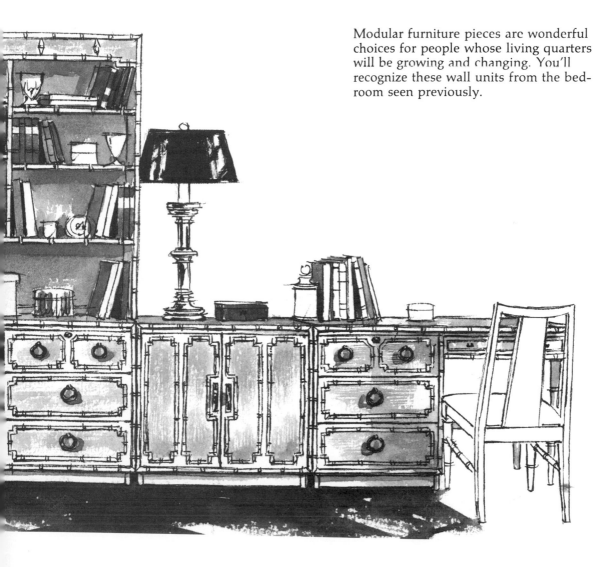

Modular furniture pieces are wonderful choices for people whose living quarters will be growing and changing. You'll recognize these wall units from the bedroom seen previously.

"Welcome—snuggle down and stay awhile! People live here who laugh and hug and listen to each other's problems. . . ."

simple wooden cubes to act as platforms to hold mattresses or plump cushions to make a windowseat or settee, or low tables that hold just about everything.

There's no end to the items you can piece together to create a pleasing look. Put trays on wicker baskets and presto chango—charming makeshift tables. Or take a circle of plywood, screw in four legs (many of these items are at lumber or large hardware stores), cover with a cloth that's long enough to touch the floor—and what a pretty dining room table!

Or save attractive jugs and bottles, then transform them into lamps by using kits from hardware or electrical supply stores or the dime store. Create keepsakes out of castoffs: glamorize old chairs and tables and bureaus by stripping and staining, or brightening up with new coats of paint. Keep your eyes open everywhere—in thrift shops and at country auctions—for those items that might not seem like much to others, but that can fill out and spruce up that very corner that "needs something" until you move or expand or are financially able to buy another quality piece of furniture. It's easy to be ingenious and, oh, what a good time you'll have seeing what decorating idea you can devise next!

Make the most of every area. If it's your first home or apartment and space is limited (or if your rooms are growing *down* because the kids have left home and you're moving to smaller quarters), make one room double as guest room and den, or

hobby room and spare room, or even living room and guest room. It's easy to make a "chameleon room" by utilizing a sofa bed or wall bed, or by building in platform beds or bunk beds.

More and more manufacturers today are making furniture that serves dual purposes. There are tables with clever mechanisms to raise them from coffee-table low to dining-table high (and then roll away against a wall to make room for a pull-out sofa bed). Other tables, carts, and chairs are made to roll around to give you a cozy conversation area during the day and then slide off into hall or entryway when you need to make room for other activities. It's amazing how functional even a funny little area can be when you put your mind to it.

Constantly keep reevaluating. And dreaming and creating. Maybe your family's growing, your budget's bigger, you've moved into a new and larger house. Or stayed happily in the old one. But however your life's changed, as time passes look at your rooms with a fresh eye. Keep a "decorating game plan" in mind: If you've chosen one of the decors we talked about, check to see what touches you can add to continue to round out your dream.

Keep updating, evaluating . . . appreciating! Maybe your room arrangements and accessories served a good purpose when you were just married, or had a toddler or teenagers, or lived happily alone. But now things may well be different, and call for different functions, needs, moods. And there are probably new furnishings, wall and floor coverings, lamps and other decorating aids on the market that you might like to add to your surroundings. At each stage of your decorating life, look at current magazines and books, go browsing around to see what's the latest.

Talk things over with family and friends. Encourage others who live with you to check out their surroundings and think what would update them and make them more appealing. Weed out belongings, groupings, even colors that just don't represent how you feel *now*. Make some immediate changes to lift your spirits. Paint a wall, switch some furniture, bring in some delightful new pictures or mirrors or candles, use a tried-and-true piece of furniture for something completely different (an old china cabinet or secretary could be converted to a serviceable bookcase or display place for plants). If the carpet's worn in heavy traffic areas, get a colorful new area rug, or move a rug from another part of the house. In other words, over the years, keep looking and wondering and experimenting. And being thankful again and again for all the bountiful blessings you've got.

Let the sky be your limit. And I'm not just talking about financial expenditures. I'm talking about all the wonderful new nooks and crannies and skylights and additions that can be a part of your life with some work and time and imagination. You might want to finish an attic that's sitting idle or a basement or garage that's clogged with odds and ends you seem never to use. Or what about turning your basement into a family room? More magic: Make a porch into a den by adding insulated windows; or transform a porch into a greenhouse. All of these things can be done with a little know-how and a lot of enthusiasm.

Or you might want to remove a wall and make two smaller rooms into one big one—or do the opposite and break a roomy space into cozier, smaller areas. If you're likely to have guests a lot, or may be having parents moving in, convert part of your house into separate quarters in which people who visit or live there can have their own bathroom, maybe even their own kitchen. (I created this sort of "suite" in my own home, and many treasured friends and guests have stayed there—including Corrie ten Boom, whom I was proud to have in my home for three precious weeks.) There's nothing quite as wonderful as having a place where loved ones can *really* settle in and feel completely at home—and have their own breakfasts or before-bedtime cocoa at their own pace, in their own privacy, just when they wish.

I'm so glad that our lives are always *changing* and that we're always learning and growing and have the chance to try new things! Oh, I *was* sorry when my own children grew up and moved out. I certainly missed them, but then there were grandchildren coming to visit, and I wanted *them* to have nice rooms to stay in. And when my grandchildren aren't there, that opens up space for friends to enjoy. And if you don't have your own children and grandchildren coming and going, there are always the children of others around to stir up a lot of joy in your life.

As the circumstances of your life change, as those you love grow up and move on, as you get a new job or a new house or a new perspective on life, as you need bigger space or smaller space or just a space that's *different*—*go* with the excitement of it all. And with each new stage in your life, with each new room you add or restructure, there's more decorating to do! What could be more exciting? There's no end to the additions you can make to add more wonder and satisfaction to your life. And I'll give you a marvelous example of just how far you can go.

My husband Dave and I loved the small cottage we lived in for years, but finally the day came when there just wasn't enough room for all the wonderful people we wanted to have come visit us. So we looked and looked until we finally found an old English-style house of weathered stone nestled in three acres of peaceful woods. A creek meandered its gentle path across the property. I loved this place as soon as I saw it. But the "clincher" came from the elderly widow who had owned the house and had raised her family there. "It has been a happy home," she said. That was all I needed to hear. I could *feel* the spirit of love in that place!

For our needs, though, we had to do a lot of remodeling. We took out walls and added a redwood deck and cozy fireplaces and enlarged certain areas. And *then* came the most mar-

velous addition of all, I get a shiver just thinking about it.

Our architect suggested we build a little gazebo on our property, in the tangle of lovely Texas trees just across the stream. But without a pause I blurted out something that surprised even me. "I want a chapel," I said. The conscious thought hadn't been in my mind before. But instantly I knew that the idea was right as right could be. I wanted "a little brown church in the wildwood" where I, or anyone else who visited here, could go to sit quietly with God, to rest and feel God's presence in the rustling of the leaves and the singing of the birds.

Today that little chapel has been visited by countless numbers of people who have slipped away from my house for a moment of prayer, or worship, or simply a quiet time with the Lord. My "Chapel in the Wood" has a stained-glass rose window and antique prayer chairs from a French convent; there are cushions needle-pointed in radiant rich colors by beloved friends. I can't tell you the peace that floods my heart when I go there. And I rejoice in the words lettered on the chapel's front wall—they're from Jeremiah 9:23, 24:

Thus saith the Lord, Let not the wise man glory in his wisdom, neither let the mighty man glory in his might, let not the rich man glory in his riches: But let him that glorieth glory in this, that he understandeth and knoweth me, that I am the Lord which exercise lovingkindness, judgment, and righteousness, in the earth: for in these things I delight, saith the Lord.

Mimsy copyright © Katzenbach & Warren, Inc.

Now It's Up to You

12

It's your turn! Now that you've read about and seen all the glorious things that can be done to decorate your home with love, it's time to start recreating God's beauty in your own surroundings. And that brings up ten two-letter words that can change your life: *If it is to be, it is up to me.*

If you want your home to radiate comfort, warmth, happiness, love—well, only *you* can do it. Only you can bring those special touches that mean so much personally to those around you. Who else knows what colors make your family smile, what flowers make your friends sigh as they sink their noses into a bouquet, what pictures or plates or pillows seem to literally "pump them up" with pleasure? Many times I've seen homes where big-name decorators have come in and done everything from top to bottom—and yet the look is "nobody's home." It's because those special, homey, personal touches aren't there; it looks as though nobody really *cares* about comfort, stimulation, delight.

And even when people do care, they sometimes live in "if only" land. "If only" I had a bigger house, or more money, or more time or imagination or energy. "If only" I were younger, or older, or brighter, or bolder. But it's *never* too late to start improving your house or apartment, and there's *always* something you can do to spark up your surroundings.

I know so many people who say they don't have enough *time* to decorate. They say they're so busy taking the kids around in car pools, or caring for older parents, or juggling jobs and volunteer work that they just can't fit in the time it takes to get paint samples or check out some fabulous new fabrics or take a look at some pretty new pictures or plaques and figure out where best to hang them. Well, you know, it says in Proverbs that "reverence for God adds hours to the day." I've been reading and teaching those words for a long time, and I can tell you for a fact they're true. If spending time with God is a priority in your life, no matter (and I'd even say *especially*) how busy you are, it's amazing how much else you can accomplish. You'll find yourself coming up with energy and ideas you never dreamed you had. And you'll find yourself living in rooms that you thought only appeared on the

pages of books and magazines.

It seems I'm constantly speaking to women's groups all over the country, encouraging women to unlock that "Special Me" that is inside them. I tell them that whether at home or on the job or in the community, they have to develop their *own* pattern for success—and I think this advice applies to decorating your home as well. So many people try to pattern themselves and their homes after what others are doing or telling them. But following someone else's standards of success will only keep you frustrated, struggling, mad at others, mad at the world. You've got to develop and trust whatever decorating timetable and tastes work for *you.*

When my children were little, I took in sewing. And I had a dress form that I used to get me started with my basic alterations. But then I had to go that next important step and fit the garment to each person individually. Some people have a bit less on the top, a bit more on the bottom and with others it's vice versa; everybody's curves are different. So for my alterations to be a success, I had to tailor each dress to each person's individual needs. It never would have worked if I had tried to put one woman's dress on another woman's body.

The same is true in creating the right look for your home. Don't ever try to squeeze yourself into someone else's pattern for success. Trust your own. Be kind to yourself. Enjoy living. Maybe sometimes you'll make the wrong decision, sometimes you'll fail—and you'll learn from it. You fail a little, you learn a little.

In the final analysis, your home should reflect *your* ideas and *your* way of life. Again and again, as my own *Home Interiors* Displayers go out around the country helping people with decorating ideas and professional tips, I make sure they understand their role is to help each woman *develop her own decorating personality.* Every woman is a decorator at heart, and all she needs is encouragement and a little know-how for that natural talent and instinct to blossom.

Scared that you can't do it? Well, I'm always telling people who seem to be lacking in self-confidence that "God doesn't take time to make a nobody." As 2 Timothy 1:7 tells us, "God hath not given us the spirit of fear; but of power, and of love, and of a sound mind." What we need in every area of our lives is boldness—and my definition of boldness is "warm confidence." It's the attitude God intends us to have toward every part of our lives, and that includes making our homes the best places they can possibly be.

So *instead of being an "if" thinker, be-come a "how" thinker.* It's wonderful what you can do with a little know-how, a little faith in yourself, and a lot of faith in God.

And that brings us to two more little words that make a big difference: *Start now.* Don't wait. Start small if necessary, and as your enthusiasm grows (and I promise you it will) so will the decorating challenges you'll want to take on. Whatever the job is, do it the very best you can, and make it shine.

My hope is that every person who visits *my* home will feel love—and I want that with all my heart for your home, too. Over the years I've learned that real wisdom is looking at others from God's point of view and sharing His love. It's an abundance that's meant to be extended—and sent spilling out and overflowing all over your home, your neighborhood, your city, your world.

"Except the Lord build the house, they labour in vain that build it," says Psalms 127:1. It's one of my husband's favorite verses. It says it all. About decorating—with love.

Glossary

Art Deco A decorating style of the 1920s and 30s with bold outlines, fluid curves, geometric shapes, and using new materials.

Baroque A large-scale and lavish decorating style of 17th and early 18th century Europe. It had ornate moldings, and bold carvings.

Bevel An edge that is cut at a slant from a main surface, often found on mirrors.

Cabriole A curved furniture leg ending in an ornamental foot.

Campaign chest A chest usually of wood, with metal corners and handles, similar to easily transported military chests of the 18th century.

Chair rail A strip of molding mounted on a wall at chair-back height to protect the wall. Often used to divide wall treatment—paneling below and paint or wallpaper above.

Chintz A fabric with a glazed finish, usually printed with a colorful floral pattern.

Chippendale, Thomas An influential 18th century English cabinetmaker, whose furniture was of excellent proportion, substantial yet graceful, and featured the cabriole leg. He worked mostly in mahogany and was noted for his woodcarving. Later in his career he used many Oriental features, hence the term *Chinese Chippendale*.

Colonial American furniture of the 18th century, usually fashioned after the popular English styles of the day. It was substantial, but more refined and stately than that of the first settlers, and is typified by the "Williamsburg" look.

Contemporary In decorating, the style that is most fashionable at any given time. At present it is functional and comfortable, characterized by a mixture of styles, old and new.

Director's chair A lightweight folding chair, with back and seat of canvas or other fabric, made popular by movie directors.

Duncan Phyfe The dominant American cabinetmaker of the early 19th century, influenced by English design, but with his own distinctive style. He worked in mahogany and is perhaps best known for his graceful, lyre-back chair.

Early American The simple, sturdy, practical furniture made by the first American settlers, circa 1620 to 1720, adapted from the furniture of their native countries.

Eclectic A mixture of furnishings from different styles and periods in the same decorating scheme.

Eighteenth century English Referred to as the "Golden Age" of English furniture design, includes the Queen Anne, Georgian, and Regency periods and the works of such trend-setting designers as the Adam brothers, Chippendale, Sheraton, and Hepplewhite.

Etagere A cabinet consisting of tiers of open shelves, used for the display of objects.

French Provincial Adaptations of court furniture of the 18th century by local cabinetmakers. The pieces were slender, graceful, and curving, and were simplified and scaled down to fit the smaller rooms of the general populace.

Gazebo A covered garden structure, usually open on the sides, popular for outdoor entertaining in summer.

Gingerbread Lavish ornamentation, characteristic of Victorian architecture and furnishings.

Gothic Heavy, carved furniture, often oak, of Gothic era (mid-12th to early-16th centuries).

Hepplewhite, George An English furniture designer of the late 18th century, whose work emphasized lightness, graceful lines, and a minimum of decoration. Furniture legs were slender, straight, and tapered.

High-tech A modern style of design making use of chrome, glass, plastics, and other industrial materials.

Ladderback chair A chair with two vertical posts connected by horizontal slats forming the back.

Mediterranean Heavy, sturdy furniture of Spanish-Mexican derivation characterized by surface carving, geometric patterns, wrought iron hardware, and embossed leather.

Modern Furniture style characterized by sleek lines, lack of ornamentation, and the use of glass, plastics, and metal.

Modular Furniture units that can be used separately or combined in various ways.

Parsons table A plain, modern square-legged table, originally made of wood and now often made of plastic.

Potpourri A mixture of dried flowers and herbs used for scent.

Queen Anne A transitional period of furniture design, from 1702 to 1714, which marked a break from the heavy, utilitarian styles of the past in favor of graceful, comfortable furniture with curved lines. A distinguishing feature is the cabriole leg.

Sconce A wall fixture holding a candle or light bulb that is decorative in nature.

Shaker Simple, well-crafted furniture, essentially without ornamentation, made by the Shakers, a religious sect first introduced into America in the late 18th century.

Sheraton, Thomas An 18th century English cabinetmaker, whose work was characterized by excellent construction, straight lines, and restraint, yet also gracefulness and refinement. He was noted for the use of inlay. Furniture legs were slender and tapered.

Stenciling A method of applying a design to rooms or furnishings by painting through an openwork pattern.

Stucco A material used to coat outside walls, and, in a finer form, to give a rough, decorative finish to interior walls.

Valance A horizontal heading, often decorative, across a window top that conceals drapery hardware.

Victorian Furnishings of the latter half of the 19th century, drawing on many styles of the past. They were heavy, elaborate, overstuffed, often formal, and yet with a homey quality.

Wainscoting Paneling on the lower part of a wall, usually topped by chair or plate rail.

Acknowledgments

The room renderings on pages 56, 57, 60, 61, 65, 141, 144–45, and 148–49 have been provided through the courtesy of Maureen Farrell, Director of Interior Design of W & J SLOANE. Special thanks to her and to the following contributors for their gracious help: Anthony C. Baxter, Vice-President, KATZENBACH & WARREN; Ann Spoor, Design Coordinator, GREEFF FABRICS; Toni Hull, Home Furnishings Manager, LAURA ASHLEY; and Peggy Heller of FPG INTERNATIONAL.

Photo Credits

Page
2 Johnny Shipman
6 E. A. McGee/FPG INT'L
10 E. Silva/FPG INT'L
11 C. Schneider/FPG INT'L (above)
    E. A. McGee/FPG INT'L (below)
14 Katzenbach & Warren, Inc.
22 S. Hogben/FPG INT'L (above)
    Greeff Fabrics, Inc. (below)
23 E. Silva/FPG INT'L
26 Greeff Fabrics, Inc.
30 Katzenbach & Warren, Inc.
31 Katzenbach & Warren, Inc.
33 E. A. McGee/FPG INT'L
34 E. A. McGee/FPG INT'L
35 M. Eckert/FPG INT'L (above)
    R. Embery/FPG INT'L (below)
38 Sloan Photography, Inc.
42–43 C. Schneider/FPG INT'L
46 Sloan Phtography, Inc.
47 R. Embery/FPG INT'L
50 Sloan Photography, Inc.
51 P. Redman/FPG INT'L
54 E. Silva/FPG INT'L
58 E. Silva/FPG INT'L
59 C. Schneider/FPG INT'L
62 C. Schneider/FPG INT'L
66 E. Silva/FPG INT'L
70 M. Eckert/FPG INT'L
71 Laura Ashley Decorator Collection
73 Sloan Photography, Inc.
74 E. Silva/FPG INT'L
75 M. Eckert/FPG INT'L
78 Hedrich-Blessing/FPG INT'L
82 Katzenbach & Warren, Inc.

Page
86 M. Eckert/FPG INT'L (above)
    E. Silva/FPG INT'L (below)
87 E. A. McGee/FPG INT'L
90 E. Silva/FPG INT'L
92 Home Interiors and Gifts
93 Home Interiors and Gifts
94 Greeff Fabrics, Inc.
95 Hedrich-Blessing/FPG INT'L
96 Home Interiors and Gifts
97 Home Interiors and Gifts
98 C. Schneider/FPG INT'L
99 E. A. McGee/FPG INT'L
102 Home Interiors and Gifts
103 Home Interiors and Gifts
106 Katzenbach & Warren, Inc.
110 E. A. McGee/FPG INT'L
111 M. Eckert/FPG INT'L
114 E. Silva/FPG INT'L
115 C. Schneider/FPG INT'L (above)
     D. Spindel/FPG INT'L (below)
118 E. Silva/FPG INT'L
122 Lisanti/FPG INT'L
123 W. Ensinger/FPG INT'L (above)
     R. Embery/FPG INT'L (below)
126 Katzenbach & Warren, Inc.
127 M. Eckert/FPG INT'L
130 Greeff Fabrics, Inc.
134 E. A. McGee/FPG INT'L
135 E. A. McGee/FPG INT'L
138 C. Schneider/FPG INT'L
142 S. Hogben/FPG INT'L
147 S. Hogben/FPG INT'L
150 P. Redman/FPG INT'L
155 Katzenbach & Warren, Inc.

An Appreciation

This book could not have been put together, or certainly come about, without the magnificent and effervescent help of

MARY ANN O'ROARK

This dear lady has a style all her own, and somehow the Lord blended us together, and she was able to interpret so much of my thoughts on the page with exuberance, with lightness, and with electricity.

And—so to Mary Ann O'Roark I give deep thanks for her everlasting help.

Edith Marie King of Regal Interiors of Dallas deserves a special mention for her eager assistance and special expertise.

Also, I want to thank the Managers of Home Interiors and Gifts who sent in many different ideas and made a great contribution to what needed to be in this book to fill the needs of Homemakers around the nation. We want it to be a book that says,

"COME ON IN—HAPPY PEOPLE LIVE HERE."